John Bowden

Who is a Christian?

SCM PRESS LTD

334 01795 5
First published 1970
by SCM Press Ltd
56 Bloomsbury Street London WC1
© *SCM Press Ltd 1970*
Printed in Great Britain by
Billing & Sons Limited
Guildford and London

scm centrebooks

Contents

Foreword

To begin with, a word of explanation is necessary. Why has the person responsible for inviting authors to contribute to the *centrebooks* series invited himself twice and not turned to someone else for the second book?

The reason is a purely practical one. *Centrebooks* have been published in conjunction with the SCM Book Club, whose members expect to receive a new title regularly, every two months. For various reasons, towards the end of the series the schedule became disrupted, and we found ourselves with a gap and no manuscript ready to fill it. To avoid the chaos that would have ensued, the present volume, an addition to the series as originally announced, was written at very short notice. Hence, among other things, the rather considerable amount of quoted matter that it contains.

The thinking outlined here has been put together and written down rapidly, but there are two ways in which it is not new. First, none of it is particularly original and it largely relies on other people's ideas. I have tried to acknowledge them where possible, but there must inevitably be some other borrowings of which I'm no longer aware. If anyone recognizes any of them, I hope he will take the credit. Secondly, most of the ideas, particularly in the second half of the book, have been tried out (and argued over) with a variety of audiences to whom I have spoken in the last two or three years. I am particularly grateful for the opportunity of giving Montgomery Lectures under the auspices of the Christian Education Movement and for the way in which it has enabled me to meet teachers from all over the country.

David Jenkins and James Richmond are the two friends

chiefly responsible for leading one who was introduced to theology through a rather narrowly biblical and historical syllabus to think about the wider issues. They will not be themselves if they do not find many faults here – but without them it would be even worse. David Jenkins was kind enough to read the typescript; his criticism and encouragement have meant a good deal.

I don't expect to write another book quite like this, so I would like it to have a threefold dedication: to my parents, with love and thanks; to Rachel, Stephen, Hugh and Rebecca, for being themselves; and to everyone at 56/58 Bloomsbury Street, my second home.

Highgate
November 1969

1 Prologue: Which is Meant to be Read

This book did not come out quite as I expected. So having reached the end, I had to scrap the original opening chapter and write a replacement. It is not that I reached different conclusions or changed my mind in midstream; rather, as I read through the manuscript afterwards, neither its general drift nor the relationship of the contents to the title emerged in quite the way I thought they might. It may therefore be a help if I try to explain what I think I have done and the sort of audience I have in mind.

This is primarily a book about ultimate questions. There are various reasons for bothering about Christianity (or any other religion): because many people in the past have thought it to be important; because it is a valuable force in holding society together and giving it purpose; because it makes us feel good and satisfies our emotional needs. But surely the only really satisfactory reason for devoting serious thought and time to Christianity is on the assumption that it is true, that it is about reality, that it tells us about how things are.

That means, I believe, that the important thing for both Christians and non-Christians is not to engage in a campaign to attack or defend the Bible, the church or what Christians are thought to believe, or to argue over a view of Christianity that might be acceptable to our particular stage in history, or even to debate the pros and cons of a way of life which has special personal associations for some people. It is to be open enough to look at religious belief and our world and our experience together: to see what belief fits in with the rest of our knowledge and experience: to see where religious belief is questioned by what we have learnt in other ways, as well as where it puts question-marks against some things that are too much taken for granted.

This, I hope, explains why a great deal of contemporary theological writing and discussion is ignored here. What I have written is a short meditation on a limited selection of ideas rather than a survey of the contemporary scene. For the more I read, the more it seems to me that much contemporary theology still has not got to the heart of the matter and will not do so unless it gives a number of begged questions a more thorough examination. I have kept to what I think are the most important issues, and left the rest. Above all, I have tried to look at some other areas in which theologians often seem completely uninterested. The last thing I want to do is to seem to be poaching on the preserves of others – theologians have a bad record of telling other people what they really mean; but so much of the ground over which religious arguments are carried on has become so narrow (and often so boring), that (as in any tolerable conversation) it only seems reasonable to talk, too, about a different set of interests.

Not that there is much hardship in doing so; personal relations, science, ethics, music, which are some of the subjects this book touches on, are all fascinating for their own sake, whether – as I wonder – they can sometimes be seen as pointers to something beyond or not. I hope it will become clear which parts of the book I have enjoyed writing most.

The line I have taken should also explain another great gap in this book. Despite its title, there is little about specific actions that Christians today ought to involve themselves in. It is said (and I imagine truly) of one Cambridge philosopher and theologian that he picked up one collection of theological essays and threw it down in disgust because there was no reference to Vietnam in the index.

Vietnam does not figure in this book, any more than the problems of race, of the inequality between rich and poor nations, of pollution, of the homeless. It is not that I do not care about these things or think them unimportant. Rather, I take the point of a previous contribution to the *centrebooks* series, Michael Keeling's *What is Right?*, that these are issues which cannot be discussed or acted on without a great many facts. As will emerge, I am more concerned with some of the forces which shape our reactions to whatever facts may confront us. The practical implications are left for the reader to draw.

Except in one instance. The title of this book is *Who is a Christian?*. One immediate answer might be 'Nobody – without being something else as well.' For it is impossible to be an officially recognized Christian without being a member of some specific church or denomination, whether, e.g. Church of England, Roman Catholic Church or Churches of Christ. Of course there are historical reasons for every division we now have, and doubtless there is much to be said against a free-for-all reunion. But when historians look back on this century, one of the most ludicrous things they will see is the combination of lengthy discussions of, e.g., liturgical revision or the finer points of intercommunion with a widespread doubt as to whether 'God' means anything at all. In more than one church, this gap between the official doctrinal and disciplinary position and what can reasonably be accepted as a possibility for belief has grown so wide that it raises acute problems of conscience – and a conspiracy of silence, if the least positively damaging course to take, is hardly enough. It would be a welcome change if this problem could be brought right out into the open.

I have ignored the fact that Christianity is, through the churches, in so fragmented a state. I have ignored, too, the fact that substantial groups would answer the question 'Who is a Christian?' in quite a specific way, in terms of definite answers, definite actions, definite commitments. I do not believe that there are any such definite answers to be had,

11

and the rest of the book will explain why. Nor do I think that there is any point in trying to draw distinctions between Christians and non-Christians for most practical purposes. We still live in a society which has been conditioned by Christianity in many ways – and if the cross-section of people one meets is anything to go by (and if the sociologists are right!) actual divisions are very blurred indeed. On the one hand, those who are unwilling to identify themselves with Christianity in any way cannot avoid its indirect influence on our whole outlook and way of life. On the other, whatever may be said for or against regular church-going, active identification with a particular religious group, such activity alone is no longer an adequate criterion for distinguishing people's *real* (as opposed to formal) beliefs and concerns.

I have written, above all, as to my friends. Some will be familiar with what I have said and will want to argue with it or perhaps to suggest how arguments might be taken further; others, who are practising Christians but are not much given to talking about what they believe, may like to see one set of cards laid on the table; others again, who are not professing Christians at all, may possibly like to look at them too.

This part of the discussion will be resumed more directly in the last chapter. What lies in between is a personal attempt to fit together into a meaningful whole a number of things which seem important in one life. The method underlying the whole book could be summed up in two pictures, produced by philosopher-theologians.

Christians do not start out without any sense of direction or without any idea of what they want to explore. Being a Christian is (in part, at least) taking a position on a particular route through a country which has to some degree been mapped already, even if at times by out-of-date methods. Some of the map may need to be redrawn as the nature of the territory can be understood more clearly and can be represented more accurately: much of it will be completely blank and will need pioneer exploration, with no guarantee that what we shall find there will always be agreeable.

> We have to make up our own minds, reviewing in the light of today's knowledge what we have inherited from our fathers. The Christian faith is a unique thing in the world, working out its development for the first and only time in history. We are, as it were, inside the first acorn that ever became an oak. How can we tell the right way to be going so as not to be an elm or a beech? When Christopher Columbus set off to sail beyond the sunset he could not tell till he got there what kind of a land he would find across the ocean. He sailed by faith and not by sight.[1]

Exploration is part of the business. But there is another element essential to religious belief that is better expressed in a slightly different way. There is not only exploration to be done, but a journey to be made with the hope of an ultimate destination. This model of the journey has been part of the fabric of Christian tradition from the story of Abraham, who (like Columbus above) is portrayed as setting out on a journey to a destination that he does not yet know, through John Bunyan's *Pilgrim's Progress*, to the present day. It has been recently used again in a modern parable:

> Two men are travelling together along a road. One of them believes that it leads to the Celestial City, the other that it leads nowhere; but since this is the only road there is, both must travel along it. Neither has been this way before; therefore neither is able to say what they will find around each corner. During their journey they meet with moments of refreshment and delight, and with moments of hardship and danger. All the time one of them thinks of his journey as a pilgrimage to the Celestial City. He interprets the pleasant parts as encouragements and the obstacles as trials of his purpose and lessons in endurance, prepared by the king of that city and designed to make of him a worthy citizen of the place when at last he arrives. The other, however, believes none of this, and sees their journey as an unavoidable and aimless ramble. Since he has no choice in the matter, he enjoys the good and endures the bad. For him there is no Celestial City to be reached, no all-encompassing purpose ordaining their journey; there is only the road itself and the luck of the road in good weather and in bad.[2]

Exploration and journeying: held side by side each stresses an important part of Christian faith. Exploration points to the need to be honest and open in our search for knowledge and understanding; journeying to the need to be committed, to the faith and hope that what we do with our life is not only to discover more about ourselves and the world around us, but to grow with all that we are and do towards a fulfilment which lies beyond what we can see.

NOTES

1. Leonard Hodgson, *For Faith and Freedom*, SCM Press 1968², p. *xi*.
2. John Hick, *Philosophy of Religion*, Prentice-Hall 1963, p. 101.

2 Pictures and Reality

If religious questions are about reality, about how things are, then at some point in asking them we shall be brought up against the problem of the nature of reality. We may not be able to say what is ultimately real, but it is possible to say a good deal about the world around us, which is the reality in which we have to spend our lives. If we are thinking about reality, that must be our starting point. Any conclusion we reach must, in the end, reckon with the facts of this world as we know them and take them into account. So first of all we must look at them and see what we can see.

Levels of Experience

In this small piece of analysis, it may help to think in terms of four different levels of experience, not completely disconnected, but each successive level taking in new elements which were not present before.

In this model, the first and most obvious experience we have to consider is that of the world of nature, the tangible, material world which the sciences help us to discover and manipulate. We cannot disregard the theoretical conclusions and practical achievements of physicists, chemists, zoologists, psychologists, sociologists; what has been said about the fabric of the universe of the behaviour of animals or the make-up of man, the whole range of modern scientific research and technology. Scientists may still be uncertain about some of their more tentative conclusions, or they may claim too much for them; they may argue with each other over many points of detail; there is still much for them to discover; but those who have split the atom and identified the DNA molecule and landed men on the moon and shown how to eliminate infections and diseases that once meant certain death demand a hearing. The success that they have achieved so far and the tangible results to which they can point give them a special authority in their sphere.

These days, however, it is hardly necessary to spend long stressing the importance of scientific knowledge and achievement. That is accepted almost without question. Indeed, it is accepted to such a degree that there is a danger that scientific knowledge may be regarded as the only respectable knowledge of reality that there can be. The problem is not so much fitting science into a picture with other levels as showing that there are other aspects of reality than the world as seen by science.

Science is essentially concerned with the world as it presents itself to the observer or manipulator, leaving him out of account as an individual person. Scientists may put forward many imaginative theories, but the touchstone of science is the set of findings which can be verified and duplicated by anyone else, given the same conditions. In this way science is impersonal, for the character or psychological make-up of the researcher has no bearing on his results, and it is universal, in that it can be translated into any social context or any language without a change in meaning.

But we are not impersonal. We are persons. It is, of course, possible to treat people impersonally, as things. Government administration has to do it, large organizations and market researchers have to do it, doctors examining or operating on patients have to do it. And it is all too common for people to be treated as things in circumstances which need not necessarily be so impersonal. Husbands treat wives, parents treat children in this way. But if we look at ourselves, we know that it is not enough. I am a person, and a person is not a thing. A person is different. I am myself, unique and irreplaceable, with feelings that can be hurt and hopes that can be fulfilled or disappointed and joys and fears and regrets and desires. And what I know

16

of myself I ought, if I were sensitive enough, to extend to those around me. Scientific knowledge is knowledge from the outside; we cannot know what it feels like to be an electron or a tree, or even a fly or a dog. But we can and do know what it feels like to be a person. We also know, in our families, among our friends and acquaintances, what personal relations – as opposed to scientific observation or manipulation – are. They, too, are part of the realities among which we live; they might be called a second level of the experience of reality.

There are, of course, people who argue that being a person and having to do with other persons (personality itself, love and friendship, and everything else that goes to make up the sphere of personal relationships) can be explained, in the end, simply as combinations of factors which can be accounted for scientifically, by the biologist, the psychologist, the sociologist and so on. That is something that we shall have to consider shortly. Until we have decisive proof to the contrary, however, we cannot ignore distinctively *personal* experience, and must take that, too, into account.

It is difficult to avoid coming up against these first two levels of experience, of the material world and the world of persons; we are surrounded by things and people all our lives. The other levels of experience that we must look at are not quite so obvious. They are also much more a subject of dispute and it is possible to go right through life without ever becoming aware of their existence.

The third level is the world opened up to us by the great creative artists: poets, dramatists, novelists, composers.

Plays, poetry, novels, music, painting can work in many ways. They can simply entertain or divert us, decorate the surroundings in which we live, like visible and audible wallpaper. They can reflect the feelings and moods of individuals and societies: sometimes synthetic feelings, sometimes deep human feelings. They can be used as propaganda, to persuade as well as to reflect. But they can also be the medium for a vision which stretches our horizons and gives us a new and deeper understanding of ourselves and the world around us.

It is possible to live and die without having, say, read John Donne or T. S. Eliot, seen Hieronymus Bosch or Picasso, heard Mozart or Mahler, or been to a play by Shakespeare or Edward Albee (to declare a few preferences!). It is very difficult to convey to others what we find in some of the works of art that speak to us; for music, poetry, painting, drama have an indirect language which does not speak in straightforward factual terms. What can be meaningful to one person can be a string of words, a confused blur of colours, a collection of discordant noises to another. We often have to become acclimatized to the language, to persevere with the unfamiliar before it begins to speak to us – and even then there is much in other people's visions that is quite inaccessible. Nevertheless, this is hardly good enough reason for ruling out the artistic vision as a constituent part, a level of our experience of reality. Those|who have found their way inside the world of music or theatre or literature or painting may argue over what they see or hear or read, but there is a remarkable consensus from audience, interpreters and creative artists themselves that they are seeing something which goes beyond the routine experience and perception of everyday life.

Finally, just as some people may never open a book, or enter a theatre, concert hall or art gallery, so too they may never enter a church or read the Bible or come into contact with those for whom religious experience is a reality to be taken into account. Religious experience is similar in many ways to experience of the world of the arts; as we shall see later, for some composers and their audiences it is difficult to tell where one ends and the other begins. Religion uses and inspires music and poetry and drama and painting as well as human living. But the heart of religious conviction is that we are not just stretching our imaginations to develop new perspectives on the world of nature and the world of human experience; it involves the further step of claiming that we and our world are not all that there is, that there is a point when the horizon opens up and gives on to a new world beyond. Religious belief is a response to what is felt to be beyond us and more than part of us. It is the belief that over, or at the heart of, all reality is God.

Pictures and their Uses

We shall come back again to these four levels of experience: of the natural world and of personal relationships, creative artistic experience and religious experience. There seems to be something in our make-up, if we allow it to express itself, which impels us to bring them together as parts of one world, to find an explanation which does justice to all of them, even if it is only the effort to explain a good deal away. The next stage, however, ought to be to look a little more closely at the way in which we do in fact experience and interpret reality (if we do) at these different levels, and try to make sense of them.

As we think, we may use arguments to clarify our ideas, we may have to resort to mathematics or even turn the work over to a computer to do it for us. But more basic than any of these methods is our tendency to react to the world around us in an essentially pictorial way. Abstract arguments are important and inevitable, but for the average person argument is secondary to a set of pictures he has in his mind. Indeed, within a formal argument, the illustrations used often remain in the mind when the substance of the argument has been misunderstood or forgotten. 'Pictures' is used here, as it will be elsewhere in this book, in a loose sense. Sometimes the pictures have a good deal of detail or take the form of a story; sometimes they are no more than a label we attach to a person or idea, or a vague assumption or feeling which has no rational form; sometimes they will be superficial words or phrases or slogans, or an association that we bring because we have been conditioned to it. A more thorough study would have to go into much greater detail about the nature of these pictures and the way in which they are related to the realities of which they are used – we should have to talk about pictures and models and metaphors and analogies – but that gets complicated, and there is not enough room in a small book like this. What I say is grossly over-simplified, but I hope it is not without a grain of truth.

We have already come across several pictures in the opening pages of this book: exploring, journeying, levels of experience. As the introduction suggested, the pictures we use can work in two opposite directions. They can open our minds to new understanding, and they can keep our minds closed so that we do not get further than the pictures we have, and never come into contact with reality at all. The pictures which open our minds are usually new to us. Some-one may be trying to explain something that has puzzled us, and we try to follow him but do not really grasp what he is saying. He tries again, with a different approach, and it is still no good. Then he hits upon an illustration; the penny drops, and everything that he said before suddenly fits neatly into place. We've got it. The pictures that close our minds are usually second-hand. As we grow up, countless pictures, labels, ideas brush off on us indirectly: from the general background of the world in which we live, from our families, schools, work, from newspapers and television. We take over these pictures without thinking much about them, and they stay at the back of our minds, to be trotted out when an occasion for them arises.

The collection of pictures that we have will be more accurate in some areas than in others, and more sophisti-cated in some areas than in others; the difference will depend very much on our education, our background and our interests. For example, we all have a vague idea of how the human body or the motor-car works, at least to the extent of knowing what to put in them to make them go; the doctor and the mechanic have a much more detailed and accurate one. We may have vague pictures of 'the civil service' or 'the common market' or 'publishing'; those involved in the day-to-day working of one of these will have a much fuller one than the stereotypes of drinking tea, paying more for food or living a gentlemanly life of leisure.

On the level of fact, our pictures tend to be neutral ones with few emotional overtones. Once a fact has been established with a reasonable degree of certainty there is no point in getting worked up over it. We only argue about what we do not know. There is little room for manoeuvre in areas where the facts have been clearly marked out. Furthermore, because our relationship with the world of things is fairly straightforward, and can without too much distortion be called 'objective', mistakes about matters of fact are either unimportant or visibly there to be corrected. I may think that Ethiopia is north-east of India, but that doesn't matter vitally unless I happen to need to go there. I may have the crudest of ideas about how my digestive system works, but that doesn't matter as long as I go to a doctor if it seems to be going badly wrong. I may think that I can keep milk indefinitely in hot weather without a refrigerator – but I will soon learn.

That does not mean that our relationship to the world around us is as simple as that of a camera or a microphone to its surroundings. We select and make sense of what we see and put an interpretation on it. The scientist often needs a helpful picture or model so that he can make further progress in his researches. Thus a report in *The Observer* in November 1969 on 'The Cancer Search' described the many models which scientists have used in attempts to throw light on the cause of cancer, and concluded:

Cancer research is a long fight to gain perspective. Soaring loftily above the daily grind of experiments, a handful of doctors insist that only a new intellectual vision will do, and that, until it is achieved, researchers will wander helplessly through the jungle of their tentative conclusions. They ask for a broader view, one that takes account of the person and not merely the cells that break down. Professor D. W. Smithers, an eminent British radiotherapist, has attacked the obscurity and contradictions of much cancer research – its obsession with an undiscovered cause that makes cells run wild, viewing cancer as a local malfunction for which a local remedy must be sought. Smithers sees it as 'a disease of organization'.

'Cancer,' he wrote in one essay, 'is no more a disease of cells than a traffic jam is a disease of cars. A lifetime of study of the internal-combustion engine would not help anyone to understand our traffic problems. The causes of congestion can be many. A traffic jam is due to a failure of the normal relationship between driven cars and their environment and can occur whether they themselves are running normally or not.'

Cancer is increasingly likely to be seen as a breakdown in the overall pattern of growth within a living system. However they approach the disease, few investigators now take the simple mechanical view that they once did. The trouble is that 'growth' is still a profound mystery. Most scientists have to take a more limited view of cancer if they are ever to get any work done. . . .[1]

Even the scientists need their evocative models for a deeper understanding.

We come next to the more complicated area of people and their nature, and the pictures we use of them. The most profound question of all in this area, 'Who am I?', will have the next chapter to itself; at this point I shall make only a few more general comments that are relevant here.

In dealing with people we come into a much more flexible area. People are much less easy to get to know than things. They change with their feelings and their surroundings, and so do we. They respond, or do not respond. There are no accepted and authoritative answers about them. They have to be lived with and worked with; and they can make life heaven or hell or anything in between. Sometimes we manage to get them right, but more often than not we get them wrong.

If we are fortunate, we shall manage to get to know, more or less, a group of people as persons, as individuals. We shall know them as themselves. But outside that group we find ourselves constantly tempted to sort people out into types and to put labels on them: working-class, student, black, German, communist, and so on. Unfortunately, when we do this, we are not just going through a process of neutral classification. Almost all the labels that we attach

22

to people also carry with them strong emotional overtones, either positively or negatively. Some are more obviously loaded than others, but there are few labels or pictures of which this is not in some way true.

There are about as many of these labels as the buttons you can buy to put on your lapel. We have labels to describe people in general, then we have labels to describe groups or individuals within the particular narrower circles in which we move; political labels for politicians, religious labels for fellow-Christians, and so on. Depending on who we are and how we have grown up, each of these designations will have connotations of either approval or disapproval.

Nor are the labels limited to people; they extend to the way in which we believe individuals or societies should live. 'Welfare state', 'means test', 'British way of life', 'freedom of speech', 'democracy' are all packed full of associations of one kind or another.

To have a wrong picture of the material world around us need not, we saw, be a very serious error; its consequences are limited. To have a picture of other people and society consisting largely of these unexamined labels is quite a different matter. For if we have to live with other people and organize a common way of life, let alone see the reality that people are, these labels are going to be a constant source of friction and prevent us from getting through to what is beneath them. For they inevitably get in our way and distort our vision. Worse still, the kind of pictures we have of other people affects the way in which we treat them. Indeed, in some societies, which operate, say, on the principle of the inequality of races, they can even turn out to be terrifyingly self-fulfilling. Treat men impersonally, as things, and that is what they will be; treat them as inferior and sub-human, and it should not be surprising if they begin to act like animals.

This is where the other pictures of man that we have are so important. For the fuller a picture of man we possess, the more we are able to grow into it and create the freedom for others to grow. It is here that the pictures from the last two levels of experience can play their part – if they can gain a hearing. But the part of us that likes to attach labels to others also has a set to attach here, so that there are barriers which some people never succeed in passing. 'Poetry', 'classical music', 'modern art', 'jazz' can be just as emotionally loaded as the labels we apply to people, and mark a closed door which is never opened so that what is behind it can be explored.

Suppose we take a particularly striking example from the world of music. Most people have heard the name of Richard Wagner. His name and his work is probably loaded with more powerful emotional overtones than anyone or anything else in music. For many, the name Wagner immediately conjures up pictures of the Nazis in pre-war Germany, and his great masterpiece *Der Ring des Nibelungen*, a massive cycle of four operas each of which requires a long evening to be performed, is regularly used as background music to film documentaries of the history of Hitler's Germany. So standard is the identification that the last chapter of a classic study, William Shirer's *Rise and Fall of the Third Reich*, is given the title of the last opera in the *Ring*, *Götterdämmerung*, 'The Twilight of the Gods'. Because of this alone the music is rejected out of hand.

Others are put off by what seems to them to be the inordinate length, the improbable plot with its repetitions and immense complications, the often turgid libretto, the dramatic setting, and the action (or often inaction). One American comedienne, Anna Russell, has had audiences in fits of laughter on countless occasions, simply telling them the plot of the *Ring*, with a few illustrations, in about twenty minutes – accurately as far as the factual details are concerned, but putting it over in such a way as to make it seem utterly ridiculous.

But a particularly perceptive music critic, introducing a full-scale study of the *Ring*, has written in rather different terms:

The quality in Wagner's music which attracts his admirers is the same quality which repels his detractors. It is not merely that the emotion it expresses is overwhelmingly human; this is equally true of Beethoven, and in the noblest sense. There are noble elements in Wagner's music; yet noble is not the word I should choose in which to sum it up. Wagner's music is not only very human, but human in a very earthy way. Against this earthiness there is set a capacity for exaltation not only of the senses but of the spirit too. In other words, Wagner touches the depths and he touches the heights. He covers the span of human experience with an impartial zest and relish which is at the very least Rabelaisian, and which those who admire him as much as I do would call Faustian.

Like Faust, Wagner was driven on to experience the best and the worst in himself until he really knew what it is like to be a human being, with a thoroughness few mortals either need or could achieve. All this experience was brought into and worked out through his music-dramas. Unfortunately for Wagner as a person, but fortunately for his art, he had a temperament which compelled him, often enough, to live out his worst and blindest side in his dealings with the outer world of men and women, but his best and most insightful side in his dealings with the inner world of visionary creativeness: i.e in his work. Not equally, however, in all his work. Whatever his *reason* touched, he illuminated, but fitfully, with a smoky glow, as he himself once realized in a rare yet somehow characteristic moment of lucidity when he described his prose writings as a poison that he had somehow to get out of his system. Whatever his *intuition* decided for him in the matter of his art, on the other, tended to be decided with real wisdom and inspiration.[2]

The content of this quotation raises a number of questions that we shall have to look at later; at the moment, the only important thing to notice is what the writer finds beneath what others find so unattractive an exterior. Nor is he alone. The crowds that try to get into any opera house where the *Ring* is performed, the sizeable public which buys the complete set of gramophone records of this sixteen-hour marathon, do so because on hearing the music they, too, get caught up in its spell and find one of the greatest of all musical experiences, reaching the heights of the human imagination.

There would be no point in writing at this length about Wagner in the present context for the sake of himself or his music alone; but in fact they make a remarkable parallel to the way in which Christian belief can be viewed from outside and experienced from within. Christianity has distasteful emotional associations of one kind or another for many people and has been associated with some very unpleasant episodes in our history. What it has to say often can seem ridiculous and even long-winded, and a great deal of amusement and a large audience can be had out of pulling it to pieces. But the fact remains that for those inside the Christian tradition there can be something far more than the superficial impressions of Christian mythology and some of the external posturings of Christians might suggest. And here, too, there is at the very least a way of looking at human existence which goes to its very depths, as well as reaching those heights that give on to another realm.

It would be wrong to push the parallel too far, but to this degree it is well worth making. It might be objected that, however hard they try, many people still do not find that Wagner speaks to them at all. Isn't this where the comparison breaks down completely – for Christianity is surely, if it is true, for everybody? But even here we ought not to be too hasty. Perhaps a better way of putting it might be that Christianity in its present form is not for everybody. For we have to reckon with the unquestionable fact that there are also many people who, however hard they try, cannot hear what Christianity is supposed to be saying.

But that line of thinking takes us off on a digression. The main point that I have tried to establish is that we still use pictures in a varied and complex way.

Christianity is not alone in its use of imagery as an approach to reality, and the more we can appreciate the way in which pictures are used in other contexts, the more we shall be able to understand both their advantages and their drawbacks at the level of religious experience.

Somehow it is usually the cruder pictures which are used as Aunt Sallies when Christianity, and particularly its conception of God, is being discussed. But even the Old Testament can counter the familiar charges:

> Have you not known? Have you not heard?
>   Has it not been told you from the beginning?
>   Have you not understood from the foundation of the earth?
> It is he who sits above the circle of the earth,
>   and its inhabitants are like grasshoppers;
>   who stretches out the heavens like a curtain,
>   and spreads them like a tent to dwell in;
> who brings princes to nought,
>   and makes the rulers of the earth as nothing.
> To whom then will you compare me,
>   that I should be like him? says the Holy One.
> Lift up your eyes on high and see:
>   who created these? (Isa. 40.21–23, 25 f. RSV)

The tradition with pictures like this two thousand five hundred years back in the past may be accused of many things, but it is hardly fair to say that it naïvely believes in a literal fashion in 'a sophisticated version of the Old Man in the sky'. Experience with such insights is at least worth probing further.

But before we go more deeply into that particular issue there is other ground that must be covered.[3]

NOTES

1. Paul Ferris, 'The Cancer Search', *The Observer Magazine* 2 November 1969, p. 66.

2. Robert Donington, *Wagner's 'Ring' and its Symbols*, Faber, 1963, pp. 28 f.

3. For a fuller discussion of religious language and the way in which it may work, see: Ian T. Ramsey, *Religious Language*, SCM Press 1967[2]; John Macquarrie, *God-Talk*, SCM Press 1967.

3   Who am I?

We have just seen how the question 'What is reality?', the exploration with which religious belief is concerned, involves dealing with a great variety of pictures, some of which may help us to see further into the truth, others of which may be hiding it from us. To examine them all is obviously beyond us. So where do we start?

At the centre, holding these pictures together, we find ourselves. But who are we? Here again we use pictures, some of which may show us more clearly what we are, others of which mislead us. And as what we are affects so much of what we see and think and believe, these pictures can shape our lives more than we might imagine. So our next question must be, 'Who am I?'

Persons and Personages

The brief answer is that we can never know. The question has been the moving force behind philosophical enquiries, novels, personal diaries, poems, plays, music. The American composer Aaron Copland once remarked that every work of art is a fresh attempt to express who we are. But how can we get at the truth when what we see is inevitably distorted, when by the time we reach the stage when we can begin to ask we have already been moulded by the whole environment to which we belong? The Swiss psychiatrist Paul Tournier puts the problem vividly:

> We are the slaves of the personage which we have invented for ourselves or which has been imposed on us by others. . . . Our personage clings to our person by dint of a long schooling which has made us what we are. It starts in the first few days of our life; it

becomes more intensive when we go to school, for school is a mould designed to standardize the human material poured into it. The child who shows originality and refuses to submit to the process is regarded as a black sheep, and thereafter he will play that role, just as his classmate will play the role of the good little boy.

Each generation of pupils passes on to the next its store of 'tips' on how to answer the various masters in the examinations; for the aim is not to give vent to personal views, but to obtain the examination certificates which are the passport into a place in society. Later we learn the sort of behaviour which will win us acceptance among our workmates, the esteem of our chief, the respect of our rivals, the appreciation of our clients, and which will hold at arm's length those whose company would harm us, while helping us to associate with those who are useful to us.

The whole of our education, our titles, honours and decorations our daily experience of life, our relationships, relatives, possessions, all go to make up our personage; they impart to it its peculiar physiognomy, and either consolidate or compromise our relations with everyone we meet. We have learnt our lesson so well that it becomes as spontaneous as a new instinct.[1]

There are some periods of history, some ways of living, some communities in which it is easier to see the problem and tackle it than in others. There are some people who, through what they have experienced or what they do or by their make up, find themselves compelled more than others to ask 'Who am I?', 'What am I here for?' We might notice that so far these questions have been easiest to raise (outside the religious world, where they are both so to speak on the syllabus) through the words of artists and a psychiatrist. On the whole, however, prosperous Western society is, on the surface at any rate, a very difficult setting indeed for asking basic, ultimate questions. There is almost a conspiracy to keep them on one side, and there is a fear that even if we look, we may not find an answer.

We are almost hypnotized into picturing the world in terms of the glossy magazines, the television commercials, the advertisements. Nice babies arrive and need to be clothed and fed and played with; they grow up into schoolboys in happy families and then become attractive consumer teenagers; they marry and make a home and improve it and have hobbies and eat and drink and meet interesting people and have children – and so life goes on and on and on. Perhaps questions like 'the poor', 'the war victims', 'the homeless', come up and stir a number of people's consciences a little of the time and a few people's consciences for more of the time; but like everything else, they are half an hour on the television; they may evoke some sort of immediate response, but on the whole they slip into the vast pool of 'world problems', about which someone ought to do something, but how intractable it all is. . . . For we are to a large degree de-humanized, only half people; the pictures that we have made for ourselves keep out too many realities.

There is no being born through pain and a mess of blood, no having joys which, unlike the synthetic ones, are all too unpredictable and fragile and fleeting and which risk being abruptly ended. There is no growing old or having nervous breakdowns; no having to come to terms with the fact that whatever the general course of the rest of the world may be, we and those whom we know and like and love are here for a short, incomplete time which will run out; no having to come to terms with failure, in our persons and in our work and in our hopes.

In our modern sort of world, the questions which the very nature of our life ought to raise for us in a profound way can be masked, deprived of their sting – on the surface – comparatively simply. They can just be brushed aside, ignored. We can pretend that they are not there, try to banish them from our minds, change the subject when they come up, not talk about them. Above all, we can blur the real issues with sentimentality. Sentimentality is a great modern substitute for religious belief, providing a sense of comfort and security without any effort. The hard facts can be given other names, the experiences can be turned into platitudes – and the nerve goes out of life. Sentimentality and religious belief can often seem very much the same, and we can fool ourselves into thinking that one is in fact the other. But sentimentality emerges as what it is when it is put alongside the realities. For instance, the modern mythology of rest and light and peace for the spirit after death as an almost automatic sequel, when what has been seen is an all too human life, illness, suffering and in the end a corpse, to be buried in the ground or burnt, may be useful as an opiate – but by itself it is hardly more than that. It has neither the heights nor the depths nor the realism of what the Christian tradition has tried to say.

But suppose we try to break through the labels and the images and the illusions and see what we really are, what will we find? If we dig too deeply, might there be nothing there at all? Is this one of the fears that sub-consciously prevents us from even beginning to try? And if we do try, where do we find ourselves on any firm ground?

Personality and the Scientists

Science might seem an obvious place to begin. But science has some disturbing questions to ask in return:

Recent developments in molecular biology suggest that we best understand life in terms of the molecular structure of what are regarded as the units of living matter, the structure of what is called the DNA molecule, the molecule of deoxyribonucleic acid. This is a molecule which is pictured as one of those iron spiral staircases which we may still find in some old houses and libraries. This DNA molecule is regarded as the building unit of living matter and it enables us to see (we are told) how, with a molecule of sufficient complexity, and of this structure, genetic development can be understood. Already it seems clear that there is in principle no ultimate gap between living and non-living matter – and that the possibility of matter being organized in the forms we call 'living' was logically implicit in the molecular properties of all matter from the start. What, then, is distinctive about human personality except its particular complex molecular organization?

Again, geneticists point out that what are sometimes supposed to be the most characteristic features of human behaviour, e.g. economic competition and progress, or the ability to do pure mathematics, may well arise from properties and capacities which have been strongly favoured by selection. Indeed, does human behaviour differ from that of animals such as horses, dogs and monkeys in any other

31

way than that it is admittedly more complex? Are the best people merely those who on the basis of a most complicated genetic development have been most successfully 'house-trained'?

Yet again we may recall how developments in neuro-surgery seem to revolutionize our views of experience and personality. . . . Memory may be scientifically improved beyond all expectation; pleasure sensations may be vastly increased at will; frontal leucotomy may lead to a zest for life which sits loose to all conventions.

These are not the only points at which contemporary science challenges a traditional account of human personality, and of the significance of human behaviour. . . . There are, for instance, developments in cybernetics where important and illuminating comparisons are made between the human brain and electronic calculating machines, so that man is thought of as a complex computer; there are developments in biochemistry and psychiatry which claim to revolutionize our views about wrong-doing and behaviour.[2]

These pictures – spiral staircases linking together to form matter, man as the sophisticated monkey, man as the programmed and programmable computer, are rapidly undergoing the development that we have already noticed. From being illuminating pictures and parallels prompting new lines of investigation they are rapidly developing into the new dogmas of a scientific age. They are fresh, and basically simple, and appeal to assumptions that are gradually being established below the level of our sub-conscious minds in the same way as Christianity appealed to a civilization that was already conditioned to think in the terms in which it was presented. Whether Fred Hoyle is talking of man as a 'a complex electronic computer'[3] or Desmond Morris of *The Naked Ape* and *The Human Zoo*, or Robert Ardrey of *The Territorial Imperative* which 'is the biological law on which we have founded our edifices of human morality',[4] or Konrad Lorenz of the 'innate aggressiveness in man',[5] there is a degree of authority and attractiveness and truth in their remarks which are quite enough to give them the potential of a new gospel.

Such an interpretation of man may indeed seem to be good news – and it is not hard to see why, even if the reason is not always explicitly recognized. The appeal of the works of Ardrey and Lorenz, for example, has been explained like this:

> In a world in which hostility and aggression seem to be a part of every man's nature, in which individual and group violence seem to constitute the incontrovertible evidence of the mark of Cain that every man carries with him, it is very gratifying to be told that this is indeed so; for those who are ready to grasp at such an explanation of human aggression it provides relief for that heavy burden of guilt most individuals carry about with them for being as they are. If one is born innately aggressive, then one cannot be blamed for being so. One can try not to be nasty, and even though nastiness does express itself one cannot be held responsible, for who can successfully resist the pressure of so powerful an 'instinct' as aggression? Hence when books such as those of Ardrey and Lorenz appear they are welcomed with all the fervour of a sinner seeking absolution for his sins.[6]

But is it true? Is it a case of: know that we are really only very complicated machines, that much of what puzzles us and frustrates us is that we are still in the grasp of our animal past and we shall have reached the explanation of the nature of man? For all its superficial attractiveness, such a solution is not adequate nor is it endorsed even among scientists themselves. Materialist philosophies show themselves in the end incapable of interpreting satisfactorily all the facets of human experience;[7] the theories of the zoologists and ethologists like Morris, Ardrey and Lorenz have come under devastating criticism from other specialists in their own field.[8] They may be best-sellers; whether they are right is a very different matter.

We are therefore driven to go beyond what the scientists have to say. Again, we cannot ignore it or try to dismiss it altogether; but we do have to ask, 'Is personality *wholly and exhaustively*, and even if only *in principle*, treatable by science?'[9] In this way we return to the world of ourselves and our pictures of ourselves and each other; we cannot by-pass them or find a solution to them through the 'objectivity' of science; we have to look at them on a personal level.

How, then, do we go behind the pictures we have of ourselves and each other in personal terms and see what is really there?

If we are ourselves so conditioned that what we have been made affects what we see around us, if our first need is for greater self-awareness so that we know what to allow for in our judgments, might not the answer be to look inside ourselves to see what we are? Self-examination has been, and is, on the lists of requirements of many philosophies and religions, and has been embarked on by numerous authors in autobiographical writings.

But I wonder whether this approach is really helpful, and not least because probably a majority find themselves constitutionally incapable of it or completely frustrated by it. 'I am thirty-six,' wrote André Gide in his *Journal*, 'and I do not know yet whether I am miserly or prodigal, sober or gluttonous.' St Francis de Sales summed up the difficulty: 'You are afraid of being afraid, then you are afraid of being afraid of being afraid. Some vexation vexes you, and then you are vexed at being vexed by that vexation.'[10] Trying to look into ourselves by ourselves leads to interminable complications, takes us further and further away from natural reactions to our situation and the people around us, and in the end can surely only result in building up yet another false picture of ourselves. Anyone who knows an over-conscientious, 'scrupulous' person will have noticed how this excessive self-concern puts a barrier round them and prevents them from becoming what they might be. The long Christian tradition of 'spiritual advisors' and modern psychiatry with its awareness of the great dangers of 'amateur psychology' both recognize quite clearly the pitfalls of too much isolated introspection.

But that does not mean that self-awareness is completely unnecessary or undesirable; nor does it mean that we should be quite unconcerned with the findings of psychologists, provided that we know how much we do not know. There are a number of established facts about what changes in the body brought about by illness or ageing can do to our personalities; there are also well-founded interpretations of certain patterns of behaviour, which are not at all what they appear on the surface and to which we should not react as the circumstances seem to demand. Even a simple realization of this can be a help and an assurance when we have difficulties or are hurt in some of our personal encounters. And, of course, some idea of what goes to shape a growing child can help us to see how best children may be brought up to give them a real chance of being themselves.

The real key to seeing who we are, however, lies – I am sure – in our meeting with other people. Not in purely formal meetings, when what Paul Tournier called the 'personage' is set up and put face to face with the opposing personage, but when real contact is made, when we are really speaking *together*. It is when we are so aware of the other person that we feel 'Now I'm beginning to know him (or her) properly' that we are, I suspect, most ourselves. Paradoxically, to be ourselves we have to succeed in forgetting ourselves for the moment.

These times of self-awareness, of the awareness of others, are among the most important things that ever happen to us. We cannot predict them, we cannot manipulate them so that they come about. They just happen. Often they come when for one reason or another the routine, everyday world with which we are surrounded is interrupted; they are not quite the same as the moments of great personal crisis, when the whole world seems to break up under our feet, but moments of crisis can prepare the way for them by the change they bring about in us.

I do not propose to go into much detail about these moments of personal encounter; they do not go into words very readily. Either you will know what I am trying to talk about or not. Our natural tendency, in fact, is to be slightly embarrassed and reticent about talking about them too much, as if we had been somehow caught naked, or as if they were so fragile that we might damage them. If the first of these feelings means that we push our flashes of deeper understanding on one side and do nothing about them, let them have no effect on the rest of our lives, then we are turning our backs on the centre of our humanness; but the second reaction seems a right one. For if an attempt is made to force intimacy, to probe too deeply at the wrong time, to improve upon it, the result can be an unbearable invasion of privacy, which is something else that we must have.

It is from here that we will be able to build up a truer picture of what we and others – particularly others – are. And it is by thinking about what these moments begin to disclose that we can develop our picture further, replacing the artificial and second-hand pictures with which we are burdened. Because our moments of real personal awareness are so fragmentary and our attitudes determined in so many ways, we shall relapse regularly; the best that we can do is to keep ourselves as open as possible for really seeing and listening to and understanding whoever we next meet. There are ways of doing this, of schooling ourselves in a new direction, but again, there is a danger. As soon as we use others as means to our own ends, exploit these moments with a view to something else, we lose what is most integral to them.

History and the Arts

We may be able to become more ourselves, stretch ourselves to the full, simply by the work that we do, whether it is a matter of consciously developing our understanding through experience and continued study or by losing ourselves completely in the needs of others. The problem comes when neither of these things is possible. In that case we shall have to look for other ways of self-expression. Music, art, literature all offer a depth of experience which we could never find in the world around us, and, as we saw, can supply us with new pictures, new ways of looking at human experience to counteract the de-humanizing tendencies of modern technology.

Above all, to understand who we are we need a sense of

history. It sometimes seems that there is a belief now that nothing that happened before 1945, or 1900, or 1789 (depending on how old and how sophisticated one may be) is worth bothering about. There is a feeling that there never was anything quite like modern man and that what he says and believes and claims is somehow an absolute. But other people have thought that before us, and have been proved ludicrously wrong. The most perceptive thinkers and writers about the past have shown that there are no absolutes of this kind, nor are the discontinuities as great as those who would want to claim them would like to imagine.

There are two important things to remember: one negative, one more positive. First, everything: religious and philosophical systems, legal codes and moral principles, the culture, social development and life of people in different ages, is conditioned by the historical circumstances in which it arose. This has far-reaching consequences, especially for our own understanding:

> We can understand, for example, Aquinas and Dante, but we cannot argue with them. Let St Thomas ask us to define anything – for example the natural law – let him ask us to tell him what it *is*. We cannot do it. But, given time enough we can relate for him its history. We can tell him what varied forms the natural law has assumed up till now. Historical-mindedness is so much a pre-conception of modern thought that we can identify a particular thing only by pointing to the various things it successively was before it became that thing which it will presently cease to be.[11]

Of course the statement is exaggerated – but it has a lot of truth in it, and we shall have to cope in later chapters with its consequences as they affect the Christian tradition.

The more positive point to be made is this. At the same time, when we read works from the past, even the very distant past, we can recognize in them, for all the different assumptions, a note of human experience which we may discover to be like our own. Nor need it necessarily be inferior.

Just as it is easy enough to project our own assumptions and feelings and prejudices on to other people around us, so it is easy to project a modern view of the world on to the past and pretend that past generations were, in comparison with ourselves, ignorant, unenlightened, barbaric. But is this really the case? And can we claim for our own particular perspective on the world an all-encompassing authority; can we explain away everything that others in the past saw about reality and translate it into our own terms? Might others not have seen something which our particular historical environment and conditioning has made us incapable of seeing but which is nevertheless true? Here is a wealth of material which, if rightly used, can deepen our understanding of humanness.

Again, an illustration from music may bring out this importance of art and historical understanding in our concern for who and what we are:

Machine civilization prides itself on its efficiency. Paradoxically it is inefficient at the only thing that is worth while – at making it possible for people to live creative lives. It does rather seem that we have purchased our increased scientific lucidity at the expense of our emotional coherence; and that it is the emotional mushiness, incompetence and dishonesty of most people's lives that we find reflected in the characteristic technical incompetence of commercial dance music, concert arrangements, restaurant music, even the 'sheet' arrangements of popular dance tunes. It is instructive to contrast the claims made on the covers for the 'melodic and modern masterpieces' of jazz pianism with the tame ineptitude of the contents from the standpoint of any second- or even third-rate professional musician.

This technical incompetence involves the decay of any sense of values. If you don't know clearly what your feelings are, if you confuse them with other feelings which your ears and eyes are all the time told you ought to feel, how can you expect to know which feelings, thoughts and modes of behaviour you consider more valuable than others? The use of propaganda in the Third Reich was only an extreme example of a general tendency. And that being so, what is the use of competence anyway? Some like one thing, and some another. All one wants is something called Entertainment; without a sense of values what can that be but the phenomenon so inappositely termed 'Variety'?

Not that there is anything wrong with wanting entertainment; what is peculiar to our time is the notion that Entertainment and

Values are distinct. How odd that would have seemed to Byrd, whose music was for people to entertain *themselves* with as they played it, or to praise God with; how odd it would have seemed to Mozart, whose symphonies differed from his divertimenti and cassations only in degree, not kind; or even to Offenbach, who remained an artist however entertaining, because his entertainment was creation, and therefore kept alive the human spirit instead of stifling it. . . .[12]

Those words were written twenty years ago, and in fairness to Bob Dylan, the Beatles or the Rolling Stones, it ought to be pointed out that the writer's verdict hardly applies to them. There is more of an answer to the question 'Who am I?' in their music and lyrics than in most of the hymns that are sung in churches. But the main argument is valid enough, and could be illustrated in other ways as well.

Towards an Answer

The nearest, then, that this chapter gets to answering the question that forms its title is in saying that we are persons, who need to be allowed to grow into what we sometimes see that we are, and who in our present world need all the imaginative insight and openness that we can acquire. That is a practical answer. But it still fails to get right to the ultimate question. What we still have not considered might be put like this.

Religious belief has had as its concern the questions 'Who am I?', 'Where am I going?', 'What is going to happen to me?', and has asked them more often than not in rather egotistical terms. In reaction to this, the modern retort has been, in effect, 'Don't be so self-concerned. Stop worrying about what is going to happen to you in the end and do something about the needs of the people around you. That is far more important.' But suppose we put the question in a different way: my friends, my acquaintances, my family, those who I know and love – and all those who I do not know but of whose fate I am aware – who are they, what is going to happen to them? Can we be as unconcerned for the future of others as we sometimes seem to be able to be for ourselves, at least, without deliberately closing our minds to issues which cry out to be raised?

In this light, asking questions for and about others, we might go on to consider: those moments of personal contact, the relationships we have made, our awareness of the richness of human experience and of the world around us, past and present, the visions of the artistic imagination – are they just here and then gone, moments of light in a great process which is otherwise meaningless? And if they are, is it worth the anguish of being hurt to expose ourselves to love, to joy, to being involved?

If that really is the case, then all that we can do is to protest – hopelessly and agonizingly – or escape. And as few have the courage to do the former at all consistently, it has to be the latter. We

turn to various forms of Oriental monism or simply to various techniques of escape, yoga and the like, which can be detached from their attendant and consequent philosophy and be used very like drugs. We are an insoluble problem to ourselves and therefore we must practise techniques which enable us to cease to be aware of ourselves or even follow out a philosophy and practice which will ultimately set us free from being selves at all. Clearly this is, in the most literal sense, the absolute contradiction of that direction and activity of the self which has produced science and technology. The thinking, analyzing, organizing and practising self and all its achievements of knowledge about the universe and consequent power to better so many of the aspects of man's life in the universe has got to be eschewed and got rid of. We are to return to the oblivion of the womb, of not being a self, and to turn our backs decisively on all the achievements, possibilities and responsibilities of human living in a universe patient of scientific and technological manipulation. Such a personal choice, to deny and reject the opportunities and responsibilities of being a person, is clearly an acknowledgement of the total bankruptcy of man. The point of being human is to cease to be human.[13]

Are we strong enough to continue as persons by ourselves? Much more to the point, is it in fact true that we are left to be persons by ourselves? Do we in fact need something more, not as a psychological projection to fulfil our personal and emotional needs, nor as a glue to cement everything together and to fill up the gaps, but because as a matter of fact there is something more and we cannot make sense of the whole picture without it ?[14]

NOTES

1. Paul Tournier, *The Meaning of Persons*, SCM Press 1957, pp. 32 f.

2. I. T. Ramsey (ed.), *Biology and Personality*, Basil Blackwell 1965, pp. 1 f.

3. Fred Hoyle, *Man in the Universe*, Columbia University Press 1966, p. 31.

4. Robert Ardrey, *The Territorial Imperative*, Collins 1967, p. 351.

5. Konrad Lorenz, *On Aggression*, Methuen 1966.

6. M. F. Ashley Montagu, *Man and Aggression*, Oxford University Press 1968, p. xiii.

7. See e.g. J. J. C. Smart, *Philosophy and Scientific Realism*, Routledge and Kegan Paul 1963, pp. 152 ff. on values.

8. See especially M. F. Ashley Montagu (ed.), *Man and Aggression* ; J. Lewis and B. Towers, *Naked Ape or Homo Sapiens?*, Garnstone Press 1969.

9. I. T. Ramsey, *op. cit.*, p. 2.

10. Both quoted by Paul Tournier, *The Meaning of Persons*, pp. 68 f.

11. Carl Becker, *The Heavenly City of the Eighteenth Century Philosophers*, Yale University Press, p. 19.

12. Wilfred Mellers, *Music and Society*, Dobson 1950, pp. 20 f.

13. David Jenkins, *The Glory of Man*, SCM Press 1967, pp. 72 f.

14. For further discussion of the questions raised here, see: Paul Tournier, *The Meaning of Persons*; David Jenkins, *What is Man?*, SCM Press 1970.

4 Beyond the World around Us

This chapter has a very modest purpose. It does not set out to prove anything (not that the book as a whole does). It is no more than a brief attempt to look at four areas in which men have believed, and have not altogether ceased to believe, that they are confronted with something that goes beyond the material and personal world that we experience; that there is something more than ourselves, those with whom we live and our physical environment. There are others who believe that the contents of each part of this chapter can be translated into quite different terms, and it would certainly be impossible to provide grounds that 'they would be prepared to accept for thinking to the contrary. Nevertheless, there may be strands here which, even if no single one is capable of taking much weight by itself, can be combined together into something stronger.

Religious Experience

Even now, for all the advances of science and modern dissuasions to belief, we live in a world of many religions. Immigration, as well as the greater knowledge of other countries and traditions brought to us by television and writing, has made this an inescapable fact. Not only do we read of Sikhs and Hindus and Moslems and Buddhists and see their religious festivals on film, but their children are with ours in school and the parents are also members of our society. They, too, have their interpretations of the world and of reality; they, too, have their traditions and their histories, and their belief that in their religious experience they are concerned with more than the material world around them.

It would, of course, be possible to write them off as people with whom the modern world has not yet caught up, who will change and find themselves face to face with crisis when the technological revolution has them well within its grasp. They can be disregarded in the same way as the past Christian tradition can be disregarded. But is this an attitude which does full justice to them? Can all that they, too, believe and claim be completely translated into other terms? Can all their religious belief and concern be explained away as social or cultural conditioning?

This is no mere academic question in our present world. The issues go far deeper. For how we understand the nature of religious belief may have far-reaching effects not only in personal, but also in social and international concerns. It is all very well, as often tends to be the case in our secular Western society, to understand religion as merely a by-product of culture, a poetic way of expressing the concerns and values of a particular group. But it makes more sense to the average adherent of one of the world religions to see religion as the foundation of culture, the element that determines its forms. Culture is shaped by a people's fundamental beliefs and values. Their attitude towards nature, man, history and the divine determines their view of the family, the state, the economic order, art and science.[1]

It is sometimes held that religion is merely a private affair, an optional department of life, which ought not to obtrude into more important matters. It is asserted that we can get on with the business of reducing international tensions, implementing economic development and technical advance without muddying the waters with such extraneous issues as religious faith and practice. But this is yet another example of that Western arrogance which Asians and Africans have come so to detest. It is the assumption that other peoples must understand and solve the problems of world community in the same way as we Westerners do. We tend to divide life into two spheres, the religious and the secular, and we assume that other peoples do the same or ought to as they become more civilized.

But peoples in non-Western cultures view the relation of religion to the rest of culture in a way quite different from that suggested above. They see religion as integrally related to and inseparable

43

from all the other areas of life and experience. As a matter of fact they generally look upon their religion as the basis of their culture, that which gives form and meaning to the whole. So the peoples of Asia and Africa are not willing to disregard their religious convictions and practices in order to get on with other matters. They see their growing independence as an opportunity to reaffirm and revitalize their religious traditions as the basis of their national and cultural integrity.[2]

So even if we wish, we are not likely to be allowed to get away with writing off the religious experience of others. Not that there seems any urgent desire to do so. One of the remarkable changes noticed in schools, colleges and universities is the rapid growth of interest in comparative religion; not necessarily to probe deeply into the truth of other religious approaches, but to see what other options are offered, how people have in fact engaged in religious behaviour in the past and how they express their membership of other religious traditions today. Some students even find themselves, rather to their surprise, seeing Christianity in a new and more attractive perspective at the end of a course in comparative religion – but that is by the way.

However, that interest in other religions is increasing does not of itself mean that they are true, nor does the increasing stress on the place of religion in growing nationalism, as mentioned in the quotation above. Nevertheless, it ought to make us stop and think, and perhaps even look a little closer. Here, a little first-hand testimony, given by a Roman Catholic monk, may speak more than a good deal of abstract theorizing.

Klaus Klostermaier left Europe to spend two years in Vrindaban, a popular pilgrimage centre in Northern India, 'the place where Lord Krishna romped with the milkmaids and fell in love with Radha'.[3] He remained there when other missionaries left to escape the immense heat because of his fascination with the people he met, the way in which they lived, and what they believed. He met and came to know a kaleidoscopic variety of characters, and talked, or did not talk, of the profoundest things:

How little we are concerned with God when we speak of God – how much we put ourselves in the limelight, even here. . . . I was to have many deep encounters, but we rarely, if at all, spoke of God. Strangely, my friends whom I thus met also told me that, if we sat together silently, they often understood more than if we talked.[4]

But of all the people he met, the one with whom he seems to have had most affinity was Swami Yogananda Tirtha, who become almost a brother to him. As their acquaintance and friendship grew deeper, Yogananda said something about the way in which he had left his work in Bombay to become a Samnyasi, a disciple of Shankaracharya. The account of his 'calling' is worth repeating at some length, if only for the moving way in which it is expressed:

I was indescribably glad, and exulted. I let everything just happen. My clothes, my pilgrim's staff, my drinking vessel – everything I gave away. I needed nothing. When someone had given me food and a hungry dog or a crow begged from me, I gave it to them and was happy if they accepted it. If I was presented with a piece of cloth, I passed it on to the next beggar. I was never conscious of needing anything. I felt myself at one with everything, as nature, without any plans, without any interests. I felt at one with the river along which I wandered – it flows on, carries boats and lets the children swim, allows water to be taken and poured into it; it flows on and on, considering it the most natural and self-evident thing in the world simply to love everyone and everything, and it was clear to me that love is the real and deepest essence of things. For eighteen months I trekked like this through India, here and there; I went with anyone who invited me. I thought to myself: is it not the supreme freedom to have no attachments, not even to this body that is transitory and corruptible? I decided to give up eating and drinking. I wandered along the Ganges, upward, into the Himalayas. One day, during my daily bath in the Ganges, I was again strongly overcome by this consciousness of being one with all, as if there was no difference between me and the river, as if my body would flow away into the infinite. But I resisted the temptation to let myself be carried away, and I walked on, up the mountains, into the beautiful landscape beyond Rishikesh. I wanted to 'cross' into the endless; into the ultimate freedom, into freedom from the fetters of the body. For days I wandered on, without food and without drink. I met panthers and bears – none hurt me, I had no fear. I did not meet any man in all those days. I remember that every now and then my strength left me, that I fainted away and then walked on again, as if in a dream.

I only remember that, one day, I suddenly awoke to find a sadhu of about sixty sitting near me. In his hand he held a goblet full of milk which he was trying to make me drink. I just let things happen. Without asking any questions he told me, without censure but firmly and definitely, that, in this way, I could not attain what I was striving for. I could not force union with the absolute; I would have to mature and change in a life-long endeavour. The awareness of reality would have to come about naturally, as if on its own; all we could do was to prepare the way for it. I asked him to accept me as his pupil, his chela. I was his only one. After about three weeks of life together, when I had recovered my strength, my Guru explained to me that he did not wish to tie me to him and that I was free to go and come as I pleased. The familiarity of daily life would show the foibles of each person and be a hindrance to my development. I left him with the impression of leaving a dream world, as if awakening from some kind of ecstasy. I knew that the goal I had seen in my 'delirium' was right; man should spend himself like a river, he should make it his nature to love and give; but the way I went about it was wrong. It is easy to get rid of the body physically; it is much more difficult to transform the body into an instrument of divinity.[5]

What are we to make of experience and insight like this?

It is easy to generalize about the 'other religions' and to pass judgment on them at a distance. But, as with so many things, at close contact the picture changes.

The Foundation of Morality

The argument that religion is a by-product of culture is also applied to the origin of the moral codes by which our societies are governed. And in fact this can be done with a considerable degree of plausibility. Why not leave the question of the basis of morality in the hands of the sociologist or the psychologist; a good deal of evidence suggests that they are most of the way towards an answer? Conscience, a moral sense, seems to be conditioned by our surroundings, not an inbuilt, fundamental guide.

The sociologist might say: People who live in a particular society are always under pressure to act in a way which is approved and not to act in a way which is disapproved. Society tends, say, to frown upon men sleeping with other men's wives because if adultery were general and an approved form of conduct its stability and structure would be threatened. In the same way, society tends to praise hard work and encourage honesty because in the long run these qualities benefit the life of the community. But changes in the community and its environment or its aims might (and will) alter some features of the moral code. 'Good' might therefore be translated as 'social' and 'evil' as 'anti-social', without being understood in absolute terms. Similarly, the psychologist might add: the moral judgments that we make are governed by the operation of a mechanism that was built up in our childhood. We are encouraged to perform certain types of action and rewarded in some way when we do them; we are forbidden to do other things and punished if we disobey. Our personal moral views are a complex result of the emotions and unconscious tensions to which the process leads; they are a sometimes open, sometimes devious expression of our personal make up.[6]

To see how plausible these suggestions are, we have only to look round at the wide differences in moral attitudes in societies past and present, and the way in which people we know – and we ourselves – can often be seen making their moral choices. It is hard to find a single definite moral principle that has been accepted for any length of time over a wide range of societies; even in so morally conscious a body as the church, there is as much evidence of change in moral judgments as there is of stability and permanence. And how can we be sure when we advocate a particular course of action as 'right' we are not exercising some unconscious impulse?

Nevertheless, while there is a great deal of plausibility in such a line of argument, which could, of course, be expressed in a far more sophisticated and thoroughgoing form than this, there are also reasons for thinking that it is not quite the whole story. For it has also been pointed out that while every society has its rules, there is also to be found among most people the conviction that there is some criterion beyond the rules, by which these rules themselves are judged. Cases may go, so to speak, through court after court, but even then it is still possible for someone to say that the ultimate ruling was unjust. How is this possible, if our moral standards can be explained solely in the terms that we have been considering above?

If we reflect carefully, we shall find that in making moral decisions we are sometimes confronted by claims which seem to be in the very nature of things, not just projected by us on to the world around us. 'The very notion of human responsibility and answerability, when explored in its many dimensions, implies an order which man does not create but which rather lays a demand on him.'[7]

What these fundamental claims are is, as we have seen, an extremely difficult matter to establish. A good deal has been made recently of the argument that the 'right' course of action is simply what is right in the situation, and examples have been produced in which what seems to be this 'right' course goes against all the accepted standards of our morality – or apparently so. Nevertheless, even this approach finds it difficult to be consistent in keeping solely within the bounds of the individual situation – and if we feel that some of the examples it uses are very much exceptions, our reaction is not necessarily to be mistrusted. There may be times when there are reasons for not telling the truth, keeping promises, repaying what we owe, being grateful, kind, just and so on; but when there are, are we simply exchanging one possible personal opinion for another?

Once we allow that moral values and claims are so to speak objective, part of the fabric of our make up and that of the world around us, the situation in which we find ourselves is put in a very different light. A purely material- istic interpretation is ruled out. There can be no arguing that the obvious conclusion to be drawn is that morality needs religion for its proper completion; it seems clear enough that the humanist view that ethics is not dependent on religion, but is quite autonomous, is a valid one. But, provided we do not try to prove too much, there might be a way that leads beyond ethics to something greater.[8]

The Natural World

To attempt to look for more than nature in the natural world, the scientists' own preserve, might seem to be foolish, especially when so many past attempts have come to grief. Surely here is one area where scientists ought to be allowed to have their say undisturbed?

Certainly there cannot be any more attempts to contradict the scientist in contexts where he is pursuing his own methods in answering questions that are suited to them. The lesson of the uselessness of looking for a 'God of the gaps', a divine presence in areas which science has not yet reached, ought to have been well and truly learnt. But that does not mean that the whole of nature, if looked at so to speak in a different dimension, need be ruled out of bounds.

Two questions arise here, for further thought rather than any conclusive arguments. What about natural beauty? We have touched on the beauty of man-made creative art – but what about that to which the poet or artist may respond?

It is something which he is trying to capture, some vision which often tortures and torments him, in itself always ineffable and beyond him, which he seeks to interpret and express in this one particular pattern or form of words. Is he not conscious of something having been *given* to him? Something seems to have come to him out of the heart of things, infinitely distant and far above him, which is yet a 'divine flame' within his own soul. From what, in the total environment, does it come? Those who hear or contemplate the artist's work (or surrender themselves to natural beauty in scenery or in the human form divine) are surely aware, even while they delight in it, that what they perceive is but a 'broken light' of a whole, an infinite sum or volume of beauty, more than can ever be realized or expressed, and perhaps ultimately inexpressible, ever awaiting our recognition, ever summoning us to a further vision, which is here disclosed, recognized and enjoyed in this present manifestation and embodiment. It reflects a quality in the heart of things, a reality which inheres in the environment. To those of intense aesthetic sensibility it presents itself as a *revelation*. When we first see the Jungfrau we gasp: we are in the presence of the 'supernatural'. It is not for nothing

49

that the psalm speaks of the beauty of holiness: we might speak of the holiness of beauty.[9]

The second question is slightly more complex. It is connected with accounts of the nature of man like those given in *The Naked Ape* and *The Territorial Imperative*. Are these, even in their own terms, the whole story? What about that part of man that responds to moral claims and to beauty and experiences religious feelings? Where did that evolve from?

The distinguished zoologist Sir Alister Hardy, discussing the theory of evolution, has shown that both external and internal factors operate in the selection of members of an evolving population of animals. Changes in colour, shape of body and behaviour patterns, the features which combine to camouflage an animal and make him resemble his surroundings, can, he argues, have been produced only by changes in the gene complex because of external selection. The choice will be made by the enemies of the species, who will tend to catch the less well camouflaged members and miss those with better camouflage. Environment, too, will act in a similar way as an outside selective force.[10]

There is also, however, something that comes from inside:

Terrestrial animals did not first get webbed feet and then take to the water to use them; they took to the water because competition for food on the land became too great and then those members of the population whose mutations produced webbing and gave an advantage in swimming tended to do better than those not so well equipped. I do not think it likely that mutations governing the nervous system made animals not addicted to water take to swimming – I believe that when food was short on the land the more adventurous ones took to diving into the water after fish and frogs. It was the same with adaptations for running, climbing trees, digging, flying and so on; new habits developed in the different populations according to opportunity and, as time went on, those members who by chance had slight bodily variations better suited to the new way of life tended to be more successful. But it was *not* chance, mark you, which dictated the change, but the new behaviour developed by the ever curious, exploring and initiating animals themselves. As evolution has advanced we see this behavioural element, this psychic factor, increasing in importance; as brain capacity enlarged, this behavioural kind of selection became a dominating factor and eventually led to tool-making, speech and so to modern man.[11]

One person, he concludes, may see evolution simply as the result of changes which have been brought about by random chemical mutations, selected in different ways by the ever-changing physical environment – 'a development largely based upon the properties of the carbon atom', as the President of the National Secular Society put it.[12] Others, however, may equally plausibly see it as the manifestation of a living process selecting the chemical units and pushing itself into every position that will hold it. The lectures in which this argument is worked out in full are entitled *The Living Stream* and *The Divine Flame;* and at the conclusion the author leaves no doubt as to which of the two alternatives he has outlined is the one he finds nearest to the truth: in the long process of evolution, the making of physical fire was one of the great milestones; so, too, was man's discovery of prayer, to kindle a flame that has brought him to higher and higher things.

Creative Inspiration and the Arts

Lastly, it is worth looking a little deeper at the world of the creative artist. We saw in the previous chapter that music, literature, painting could enlarge our experience of and insight into human nature; there are some who feel that at times it goes even beyond that. A sizeable anthology could be (and probably has been) made of passages in which writers, painters and composers describe the source of their inspiration. It would be likely to show how many of them feel drawn to write almost in religious terms.

Beethoven wrote to Bettina Brentano:

Tell Goethe to listen to my symphonies, for then he will admit that music is the only entrance to the higher world of knowledge which, though it embraces me, a man cannot grasp. A rhythm of the spirit is needed in order to grasp the essence of music; for music grants us presentiments, inspiration of celestial sciences, and that part of it which the mind grasps through the senses is the embodiment of

51

mental cognition. Although minds live on it, as we live on air, it is still a different thing to be able to grasp it intellectually. Yet the more the soul takes its sensuous nourishment from music, the more prepared does the mind grow for a happy understanding with it. Yet few ever attain this stage; for just as thousands marry for love and love is never manifested in these thousands, although they all practise the craft of love, so thousands have intercourse with music and never see it manifested. Like all the arts, music is founded upon the exalted symbols of the moral sense; all true invention is a moral progress. To submit to these inscrutable laws and by means of these laws to tame and guide one's mind, so that the manifestations of art may pour out: this is the isolating principle of art. To be dissolved in its manifestations, this is our dedication to the divine which calmly exercises its powers over the raging of the untamed elements and so lends to the imagination its highest effectiveness. So always art represents the divine, and the relationship of men towards art is religion; what we obtain from art comes from God, is divine inspiration which appoints an aim for human faculties, which aim we can attain.[12]

We might set alongside that some remarks by a composer from the present, Michael Tippett, as he reflected on his own aims and hopes in a radio broadcast:

Because we have starved our imaginative life of energy, we have forced it to be childish and dubious. Yet it is in this underworld that the new pictures are being made. And I for my part believe we shall see the way out more like a picture, a dream, than a blue-print. Then one day, we shall put our passion behind our picture of a new world, and bring the picture to life. . . . All enrichment, all renewal of our spiritual life will come first from persons. What matters at this moment is that I as a person speak truth to others as persons who sit in homes I shall never enter.

Truth is some sort of an absolute. If we begin to tell lies for any cause, however good, we hurt ourselves, whether we know it or not. Beauty is another absolute. When we let the common level of our social life sink away too far from the beautiful and the comely, we suffer as sharply as if we took the children's milk to make whipped cream for the wealthy. Part of the poet's, the painter's, the musician's job is just that of renewing our sense of the comely and the beautiful. If, in the music I write, I can create a world of sound wherein some, at least, of my generation can find refreshment for the inner life, then I am doing my work properly. It is a great responsibility: to try to transfigure the everyday by a touch of the everlasting, born as that always has been, and will be again, from our desire.[14]

In the second quotation the tone is more muted, the terms in which the idea is put are rather different, but there are still similarities, feelings that are expressed with more than just sentimentality in musical pieces about music itself, like Schubert's *An Die Musik* or the Composer's aria which brings the Prologue of Richard Strauss's *Ariadne on Naxos* to a close. Mere emotion? Perhaps, but might there be more?

In a still controversial account of *The Language of Music*, Deryck Cooke has begun what promises to be a fascinating enquiry into what music expresses and the way in which it expresses it. He tries to show that the idea that music can express certain quite definite things is not a romantic illusion, but has been an unconscious assumption of composers of all ages. Accounts like those quoted above can be interpreted in terms of ideas, inspiration, coming up from the composer's unconscious mind to be shaped by the creative imagination through melody, rhythm or harmony into new forms which can embody new emotions. By hearing the expression of these emotions, or by playing it ourselves, we, too, can join in the emotional content that the music was written to express:

The professional, besides apprehending the music emotionally, can analyse the form with his intellect, and can admire its formal beauty with his aesthetic sense (strange to say, these three processes can go on simultaneously); whereas the layman, unable to lay hold on the fluid, intangible sounds with his intellect, can only apprehend the music as emotion (and vaguely as formal beauty, no doubt, in an unconscious way). So that, after a performance, the professional can discuss the technical aspects of the music with one person, and its formal beauty with another, using a technical vocabulary to describe the various elements; but the layman, even though he may have more than an inkling of these things, is more or less tongue-tied for lack of technical knowledge. But when we come down to the fundamental musical experience – the transformation of the sound into emotion – the professional is as tongue-tied as the layman.[15]

So far, of course, we are still on the same ground as that covered by the previous chapter, though we may see a little more clearly how music helps us to understand ourselves more – particularly in so emotion-starved an age. But it may be possible to go even further, to a point where we see how we might talk of music going beyond our own experience, 'representing the divine'. Because this further transition is a difficult one to make, and fatally easy to overstate, it had better be hinted at, once again, in Deryck Cooke's own words:

> Whether music can express spiritual or mystical intuitions is a question that cannot at present be answered, since we have no generally established and acknowledged body of knowledge on these matters; a lack largely responsible for what Hans Keller has so rightly called 'the supreme (if unpremeditated) critical cowardice of our age ... the refusal to face the metaphysical problem'. Many people have derived experiences of this kind from music – the present writer has from the symphonies of Bruckner and Mahler – but in what way it exists in the notes is still a dark and unresolved problem. ...
>
> What seems certain is that if music does express spiritual or mystical intuitions, it must do so through the emotional terms of musical language, just as the writings of, say, St John of the Cross express his mystical experience in the emotional terms of spoken language. But with a metaphysical insight into music, we should undoubtedly experience these terms with a different kind of feeling: they would be revealed as the same but also something other, just like the sexual symbolism of some mystical writings.
>
> We may say then that, whatever else the mysterious art known as music may eventually be found to express, it is primarily and basic-ally a language of the emotions, through which we directly experience the fundamental urges that move mankind, without the need of falsifying ideas and images – words or pictures. A dangerous art, in fact, as was realized by Plato, the fathers of the mediaeval church, and Tolstoy, all of whom wished to control and confine the use of it. But under the guidance of the intellect and the enlightened moral sense, it is surely as safe as anything human can be – as safe at least, shall we say, as religion or science.[16]

Whether or not this approach is fully justified is, as was said, still being debated. But the way in which it runs parallel to other developments that we have been noting is an encouraging sign. Perhaps it is significant that in an even more recent study of 'Renewal in twentieth-century music',

54

Wilfred Mellers has drawn on the religious terms of revelation and incarnation as key themes in a fascinating and illuminating argument.[17]

To end this chapter as it began: there can be no question of proving anything here. I have done no more than suggest some pointers beyond ourselves, pointers which, taken together, may make it worth while to look further into the question of God. But even this small beginning represents an advance over the more pessimistic views which have become customary in many scientific, artistic and theological circles. We shall come up later against arguments in a different direction.

NOTES

1. For this point see Owen C. Thomas, *Attitudes Toward Other Religions*, SCM Press 1969, pp. 1 ff.

2. *Op. cit.*, pp. 2 f.

3. Klaus Klostermaier, *Hindu and Christian in Vrindaban*, SCM Press 1969, p. vii.

4. *Op. cit.*, p. 37.   5. *Op. cit.*, pp. 55 f.

6. For this paragraph see James Richmond, *Faith and Philosophy*, Hodder and Stoughton, p. 115.

7. John Macquarrie, *Three Issues in Ethics*, SCM Press 1970, who discusses this well.

8. For an attempt to argue further in this direction see H. P. Owen, *The Moral Argument for Christian Theism*, Allen and Unwin 1965.

9. F. R. Barry, *Secular and Supernatural*, SCM Press 1969, pp. 136 f.

10. This paragraph follows a short statement of his views in *Biology and Personality*, pp. 74 ff.

11. Alister Hardy, *The Divine Flame*, Collins 1966, pp. 221 f.

12. David Tribe, in *Dialogue with Doubt*, SCM Press 1967, p. 39.

13. Beethoven: *Letters, Journals and Conversations*, Cape 1951; quoted by Wilfred Mellers, *Caliban Reborn*, Gollancz 1968, pp. 30 f.

14. Michael Tippett, 'A Composer's Point of View', in *Moving into Aquarius*, Routledge and Kegan Paul 1959, pp. 11 f.

15. Deryck Cooke, *The Language of Music*, Oxford University Press, p. 205.

16. *Op. cit.*, p. 272.

17. Wilfred Mellers, *Caliban Reborn*, Gollancz 1968.

5 Prayer

'The creed of the English,' Alasdair MacIntyre has written, 'is that there is no God and that it is wise to pray to him from time to time.'[1] There is more truth in this cynical comment than might appear, but it needs to be put in a slightly different way. Many people cannot find any reason for believing in God or avoid the question of belief altogether, but are still, at some time or another, driven to pray.

Because this feeling of the need to pray is a human experience, and prayer arises in this way, the question of prayer can be raised before the question of God, and can form so to speak a bridge between the questions we have been considering so far and the question of God, the central question of all religious belief. The connection between the question of prayer and the question of God can be seen in the way in which difficulty in belief in God goes hand in hand at present with difficulty in prayer.

For it is clear that most people are finding prayer very hard, even if they have been accustomed to pray in the past, and while there are occasions when the need to pray is felt, at the same time there is a nagging suspicion that this need to pray might stem from psychological, emotional grounds and not be a pointer to anything at all.

Now whether it is the case that people find difficulty in believing in God because they do not pray, or that they do not pray because they find difficulty in believing in God is a nice point that can be argued over at great length; whichever way the argument comes out, however, there seems only one possible approach to tackling the problem. The difficulties have to be taken together, and we have to begin by exploring prayer ourselves.

But how can we pray if we find the idea almost impossible? And where do we start? This chapter outlines just one possible approach.

Preparation

Some important preliminaries to prayer have in fact already emerged from what we have looked at so far. To come to terms with who we are and with the nature of our personal relationships is one preliminary; this deeper awareness and self-awareness is itself half way to prayer. So, too, is the greater awareness that comes from the kind of reflection described in the previous chapter, on other dimensions of the world around us. It may well be that we are often near to real prayer without our being aware of it. A false picture of what prayer ought to be may be keeping us from the reality.

Colin Alves has put it like this:

We meet God in ourselves, in other people, in the world-process which surrounds us and of which we are a part, but the frightening thing remains that we can meet him without recognizing him, and in that case we have failed to achieve a meeting at all.

Earlier this year the Queen visited Winchester at a time when we were entertaining some Swedish guests. They were astonished to learn that this was the first occasion on which any member of our family had ever had an opportunity even to see the Queen in person. For them, living in Stockholm, the situation was that they might find themselves one day talking to their King in a shop, or on the street, possibly without recognizing him.

Perhaps some of the 'spiritual exercises' which we have devised in the past have been influenced by our very British view of monarchy. If we follow these disciplines, we say to ourselves, we will find the road that leads to Buckingham Palace, or it may be Windsor, or even homely Sandringham, but it will still be a special place apart to which we have to go if a meeting is to be effected. Or possibly, if we are very lucky, the royal car will pass our way, and we will have a fleeting glimpse of majesty, provided of course that we are standing in the right place on the pre-appointed route.

Could it not be that a truer form of 'spiritual exercise' would be

57

something that prepares us to *recognize* royalty when we encounter it (or rather, when it encounters us) unexpectedly in the midst of the everyday and ordinary?[2]

If one of our main problems with praying is that we tend to think in a way which excludes any 'spiritual' dimension, if our approach to the world is so literal that we are strongly tempted to dismiss any idea that there is something or someone that transcends it, then we may find it necessary to spend a good deal more time on the preparation than on the actual praying. It may be that by attempting to rush straight into prayer we are frustrating ourselves, that this is why times set aside for prayer can seem so empty.

The Beginning of Prayer

We start, then, with ourselves, and it does not matter to begin with if we are not particularly clear to whom we are praying as long as we do pray.[3] Plenty of people pray under all kinds of misconceptions. It is as we pray that we begin to clarify our ideas. Indeed, this is one of the authentic sources from which our insights grow. Perhaps we are certain to whom we pray, but even then, it may help to look more closely at the pictures that come to mind. Austin Farrer described one change of view in his praying as a young man:

I thought of myself as set over against the deity as one man faces another across a table, except that God was invisible and infinitely great. And I hoped that he might signify his presence to me by way of colloquy, but neither out of the scripture I read nor in the prayers I tried to make did any mental voice address me. . . . So I would no longer attempt, with the psalmist, 'to set God before my face'. I would see him as the underlying cause of my thinking, especially of those thoughts in which I tried to think of him. I would dare to think that sometimes my thoughts would become diaphanous, so that there might be some perception of the divine cause shining through the created effect, as a deep pool, settling into a clear tranquillity, permits me to see the spring in the bottom of it from which its waters rise. I would dare to hope that through a second cause the First Cause might be felt, when the second cause in question was itself a spirit, made in the image of the Divine Spirit, and perpetually welling up out of his creative act.[4]

One is reminded of Paul's words, 'We do not know how to pray as we ought, but the Spirit himself intercedes for us in sighs too deep for words' (Rom. 8.26).

But to begin with, we could go even further in this direction and leave out for the moment any reference to 'God'. Prayer can be seen as what comes up from within ourselves. The beginnings of prayer lie in other moments that are very real to us, when we are made particularly aware of the realities of our situation. We may be in need or distress, forced to take account of what we had thought would not affect us; we may be overwhelmed with gratitude and joy and simply want to say 'thank-you'; we may feel a longing that goes beyond anything we can have in our present world (Augustine's 'Our soul is restless until it finds rest in thee'); we may be exhausted and want to do no more than let ourselves go completely. This kind of spontaneous prayer is limited prayer, and it may be only very occasional prayer, but it is an invitation to go further; to pursue the exploration.

It would be possible to put the stress on these 'real' moments and regard anything else as secondary. There has been much talk about whether it is really desirable to set aside special times for prayer regularly; some argue that the real point of prayer comes in and with particular meetings and actions:

> I suspect we have got to ask very seriously whether we should even begin our thinking about prayer in terms of the times we 'set aside', whether prayer is primarily something we do in the 'spaces', in the moments of disengagement from the world. I wonder whether Christian prayer, prayer in the light of the Incarnation, is not to be *defined* in terms of penetration through the world to God rather than of withdrawal from the world to God. For the moment of revelation is precisely so often, in my experience, the moment of meeting and unconditional *engagement*. . . . What enlightenment I have had on decisions has almost always come not when I have gone away and stood back from them, but precisely as I have *wrestled through* all the most practical pros and cons, usually with other people. And this activity, undertaken by a Christian trusting and expecting that God is there, would seem to *be* prayer.[5]

59

But it is asking a great deal of us as persons to be able to sustain our sensitiveness, to keep our balance, to concentrate all our resources in such moments unless there is some more permanent basis on which we can rely. And it is here that the discipline of a more regular pattern of reflection and prayer comes in.

We ought to be able to enlarge our horizons, developing from our perception in what comes spontaneously to greater perception at times and in concerns when we are not affected so spontaneously; we ought to be able to go on from asking or thanking when the occasion is thrust upon us to realize other needs and occasions for asking and thanking of which we were not previously aware. All this requires time apart and time for reflection, and it is too much to expect that we shall get down to it properly unless we deliberately find room somewhere.

In face of such experience as daily life provides we are called upon to make a great many decisions, and their quality will depend to a great extent upon the 'ordering' of our attitude effected through praying. Either we respond with 'off the cuff' decisions, prompted by fears, jealousies, fads, enthusiasms, or we respond out of imaginative, sensitive, integrated, many-sided awareness of the time, event and question. Prayer that has built up a coherent, generously conceived structure for living is clearly involved in all such moments, and not least when we make some bad decisions and see others as mediocre and feeble.[6]

The difference between this kind of reflection and the self-examination mentioned in an earlier chapter is the element of sharing that is involved. 'Somehow,' writes Sir Alister Hardy, 'in some extraordinary way, I do believe that there is a vast store of wisdom and spiritual strength that we can tap in this way – something which is of the utmost importance to mankind.'

He continues:

At the *very least* I expect this power of which we speak may be some sub-conscious shared reservoir of spiritual 'know-how' which we call Divine. I think, however, it is *far more likely* that above this there is something much more wonderful to which we give the name God.

But even if it *should* be shown, and I don't believe it will, that this whole conception is a purely psychological one and, if, in some way, this mind factor *should* eventually be proved to be entirely of physico-chemical origin – it would not to my mind destroy the joy or help of *the experience we may still call Divine* any more than it would destroy the glorious beauty felt in poetry or art.[7]

But this raises urgently the question with what we are sharing our reflection, towards what our 'prayers' are directed.[8] The same issue arises in another writer, who provided one of the most surprising pieces of spiritual writing to appear over the past decade, Dag Hammarskjöld, former Secretary General of the United Nations. In *Markings*, a manuscript that was found in his New York house after his death, he wrote:

> I don't know Who – or what – put the question, I don't know when it was put. I don't even remember answering. But at some moment I did answer Yes to Someone – or Something – and from that hour I was certain that existence is meaningful and that, therefore, my life, in self-surrender, had a goal.[9]

'Who' or 'what', 'Someone' or 'Something'? What is experience in prayer experience of?

In Christian tradition, the answer has been unanimous. In reply to the question 'How do you pray to the ground of your being?', prompted by some remarks in *Honest to God*, Dr Robinson replied:

> I do not pray to the ground of my being. I pray to God as Father. Prayer, for the Christian, is the opening of oneself to that utterly gracious personal reality which Jesus could only address as 'Abba, Father'. I have no interest whatever in a God conceived in some vaguely impersonal pantheistic terms. The only God who meets my need as a Christian is 'the God of Abraham, Isaac and Jacob', the 'God and Father of our Lord Jesus Christ' – not 'the God of the philosophers', who, as Brunner once put it, 'simply allows himself to be looked at'.[10]

With these remarks, questions are raised which will only be clarified further in subsequent chapters. For the moment, the important point is the main one. In the end, the Christian tradition has not been satisfied with anything that falls short of speaking of God in personal terms. This is the only way, despite the problems it raises, of doing justice to what we begin to see as the nature of our own prayer and what we can often see more clearly in the testimony of others.

Of course, as we shall see when we consider the question of God, it is possible to object that prayer may be a looking towards an unconscious or sub-conscious invention of man to satisfy what he lacks, an invented father figure. That is an objection that has already been raised and one that we shall have to consider again briefly. There *are* arguments that can be put forward in an opposite direction. But in the end the answer must be to go on praying and to look carefully at what we are doing when we pray, and to ask whether such an explanation really does justice to what we and others seem to be doing.

Earlier in this chapter it was suggested that we may find that many traditional ways of prayer hinder rather than help. This may be so. But that does not mean that we should ignore how those in the past have prayed altogether. We shall need to look not only at the Bible itself, but also at some of the other writings on prayer written over the history of Christianity. There is a great deal of it. Much is dead beyond recall; much will only be usable with a good deal of caution and criticism. But we may well find that it says more to us and does more to stimulate our own prayers than we might imagine.

Exploring the prayers of others might seem a bit like praying at second hand, and perhaps it is. But it is important. For prayer being what it is, and we being what we are, it is inevitable that there will be numerous times when we are tempted to give it up, when we wonder whether really we are doing anything more than talking to ourselves. It is here that we may be helped by our knowledge of the way in which others have prayed – and that others are still praying. There is no one way of praying; there are many that can be tried. The important thing is that we continue with it:

Prayer is a practical possibility to be explored, and not something that can be theoretically excluded or authoritatively commanded. If it is anything, prayer is a response and a receiving. The question 'Why Pray?' is really the question 'What is there to respond to and to receive?' Prayer is acting on the faith that there is in the world and beyond the world that to respond to which can rightly be referred to only as 'He' because 'He' is personal in the sense of offering the possibility of response and desiring the realization of this response from such as us. Prayer is seeking to experience the world, and sometimes achieving the experiencing of the world, as embraced in a personal purpose and a personal possibility. Some achieve this simply by being willing to reach out from themselves to whatever there is. Others are drawn out into this search and response of prayer by the mystery encountered in personal relationships. Others are kindled to the quest by seeing in the traditions of praying that which reflects a possibility they have experienced or glimpsed or guessed at. Still others are encouraged by the simple impression of Jesus Christ. And all these ways and others intermingle variously to entice men or drive men or encourage men to pray because they have at least half a desire to respond to a felt possibility or to receive a glimpsed gift. So prayer is not primarily a useful practice, an externally obligatory practice, or a guaranteed practice, but rather an evoked response like the first gropings and the later steadfastness of love. We pray because we see we might or dare to hope we may.[11]

NOTES

1. Alasdair MacIntyre, 'God and the Theologians', in: David L. Edwards and J. A. T. Robinson (eds.), *The Honest to God Debate*, SCM Press 1963, p. 228.

2. Colin Alves, 'Spirituality and Personal Growth', in: Eric James (ed.), *Spirituality for Today*, SCM Press 1968, pp. 148 ff.

3. For a good deal of what follows I am particularly indebted to Alan Ecclestone, 'On Praying', *Spirituality for Today*, pp. 29–40, which is the best short piece of writing on prayer that I know.

4. A. M. Farrer, *The Glass of Vision*, Dacre Press 1948, pp. 7 f.

5. J. A. T. Robinson, *Honest to God*, SCM Press 1963, p. 97.

6. Alan Ecclestone, 'On Praying', *Spirituality for Today*, p. 39.

7. Alister Hardy, *The Living Stream*, Collins 1965, pp. 285, 287. I am not very happy about the context in which the remarks are made.

8. For a fuller discussion of this see Peter Baelz, *Prayer and Providence*, SCM Press 1968, pp. 38 ff.

9. Dag Hammarskjöld, *Markings*, Faber 1964, p. 169.

10. J. A. T. Robinson, *The Honest to God Debate*, pp. 261 ff.

11. David Jenkins, 'What is it to Pray?' (unpublished). Quoted by kind permission.

6 God

Despite the direction in which the three previous chapters have been pointing, they do not add up to certainty, as well we know. We looked at ourselves, and saw the person in his incompleteness pointed towards something beyond himself; we looked at the world around us, and noted some areas in which it seemed as though there might be a chance of taking a further step. We considered the nature and possibility of prayer. But it is still not a straightforward matter to go on from there to argue that there must be God, and having established that, confidently to demonstrate the reasonableness of the Christian faith, though that is a course that has been followed often enough in the past.

For to give the impression of too much confidence does not do justice either to the questionings and difficulties of so many people today, nor to the character of what belief in God I feel I might have. Nor does it seem to do justice to God, if there is God.

Believing in God is more than being led by a series of questions about ourselves and our world to say, 'There must be more'. If it is worth anything, it is, it must be, better than that – and it is something that we are left to accept or reject with a considerable degree of freedom. It is not even something that can be secured by prayer.

The Hidden God

In the first chapter of this book, when we were looking at different 'levels of experience', we saw how the possibility of argument, of conflicting opinions, grew greater as we moved towards the area of religious belief. We might now put it in another way, and say that the degree of freedom to respond grows greater as we move in this direction. God cannot be forced on us (nor does he force himself upon us) against his will – that is why the question of God is such an open one.

John Hick has written about this very well in his book *Faith and Knowledge*. If we are to be able to exist as free persons in our own right before God, then God, by virtue of his very nature, must veil himself from us. For knowing God is not just a matter of knowing yet another being who inhabits our universe. Knowing God is knowing the one who is responsible for our existence and who has our future in his hands.[1] A Jewish parable puts it in a vivid way: An emperor visited a certain rabbi, Joshua ben Hananiah. 'I should like to see your God,' he remarked. 'But that is impossible,' said the rabbi. 'But I *will* see him,' insisted the emperor. So the rabbi led him out into the sunshine during the summer solstice and said, 'Now look at that.' 'I cannot,' was the reply. 'The sun,' concluded the rabbi, 'is only one of God's servants; and you ought to admit that as you cannot look into it, much less can you behold his glory.'[2]

John Hick sums up his discussion in a profound paragraph:

To become aware of the existence of such a being must affect us in a manner to which the awareness of other human persons can offer only a remote parallel. The nearest analogy on the human level is the becoming aware of another which is at the same time a falling in love with that other. This is an awareness far removed from casual observing; in it the observer is himself profoundly involved and affected, so that the whole course of his life may thenceforth be changed. However, in all our purely human relationships the other remains ultimately on 'the same level' as ourselves, whereas in the knowledge of God the Other is one to whom the only appropriate relationship is the utter abasement of worship. In 'finding God' the worshipper abdicates from the central position in his world, recognizing that this is God's rightful place. His life must become consciously reorientated towards a Being infinitely superior to himself in worth as well as in power. There is thus involved a radical reordering of his outlook such as must be undergone willingly if it is not to crush and even destroy the personality. For so great a change can only be a conversion of the same person, and not the substitution of another person, if there is throughout a continuity, not only of memory, but also of insight and assent. Only when we ourselves *voluntarily* recognize God, desiring to enter into relationship with him, can our knowledge of him be compatible with our freedom, and so with our existence as personal beings. If God were to reveal himself to us in the coercive way in which the physical world is disclosed to us, he would thereby annihilate us as free and responsible persons. . . . If man is to be personal, God must so to speak stand back, hiding himself behind his creation, and leaving us the freedom to recognize or fail to recognize his dealings with us.[3]

Here, put in positive terms, is an explanation of that cry which has gone up so often since the days of the Second Isaiah, whose writings have made it so familiar: 'Truly, thou art a God who hidest thyself'. But they are *positive* terms, and the same position can also be described in a far more negative way. 'God is dead', runs one of the more recent popular slogans, and while it is only a slogan, and one which does not stand up to much careful analysis, it has enough in it to make it popular among some of those people who still feel that its message is true and not too obvious to be worth stating.

Another parable sets out all the difficulties:

Once upon a time two explorers came upon a clearing in the jungle. In the clearing were growing many flowers and many weeds. One explorer says, 'Some gardener must tend this plot'. The other disagrees, 'There is no gardener'. So they pitch their tents and set a watch. No gardener is ever seen. 'But perhaps he is an invisible gardener.' So they set up a barbed-wire fence. They electrify it. They patrol it with bloodhounds. (For they remember how H. G. Wells's *The Invisible Man* could be both smelt and touched, though he could not be seen.) But no shrieks ever suggest that some intruder has received a shock. No movements of the wire ever betray an invisible climber. The bloodhounds never give cry. Yet still the Believer is not convinced. 'But there is a gardener, invisible, intangible, insensible to electric shocks, a gardener who has no scent and makes no sound, a gardener who comes secretly to look after the garden which he loves.' At last the Sceptic despairs, 'But what remains of your original assertion? Just how does what you call an invisible, intangible, eternally elusive gardener differ from an imaginary gardener or even from no gardener at all?'

The question being asked is, 'What difference does God make? Where does he fit in?' And if he makes no difference, and cannot be fitted in, then why should 'God', if the word in fact means anything at all, concern us? It is one thing talking about what is 'beyond' the natural world, personality, moral awareness, appreciation of beauty and so on, but can that 'beyond' be fitted into our knowledge of our own make up and behaviour or the workings of our environment? As well as drawing a line from ourselves towards God, can we draw a line back showing how God might affect our experience and the world? Here there are some serious difficulties.

The Retreat of God

There is a history of the way in which God has gradually been forced out of the world, of how the arguments for his existence have been made more and more difficult, over the past two hundred years or so, which seems likely to become as familiar as many of the stories in the Bible. We might call it 'The Retreat of God'. Put in the simplest and crudest of terms it goes something like this (there are other more detailed and more accurate accounts available elsewhere which put the development in more technical terms and add the names of the main characters involved).

Once upon a time all Christians believed in God. It was the natural thing to do and there was no reason not to. Only a fool would think to deny God. The first steps in the rise of the modern scientific approach seemed to provide independent confirmation for the reasonableness of belief in God. Divine workmanship was seen in the bodies of animals and in plants, the muscles of a man's body and the eye of a fly; God was the one who actively kept the stars in position and determined the course of the planets.

But this harmony was not to last. Explanations were found for these wonders of nature in very different terms. More disturbing to religious claims, the whole concept of the nature of knowledge was transformed. Reason, it was argued, cannot penetrate beyond nature to unseen and hidden realities. What we know, we know from observation and experience and our interpretation of it, and we cannot argue validly from the world we know to a world that we do not and cannot know. On this basis it is possible to challenge all arguments for the existence of God from our experience of the natural world.

But what about morality? Was this not still a sure way to God? An attempt was made to fall back on morality as a second line of defence of belief in God, but this proved no stronger than the first. If science is simply science, in its own right, capable of functioning independently without involving God, why should not the same be true of morality? Right and wrong are right and wrong, whether you may happen to believe in God or not. Why drag God in this way, so to speak through the back door? As with arguments for the existence of God from our experience of the natural world, so too arguments for the existence of God from morality could all be challenged.

That leaves religious experience. We are to find God in the human consciousness, in our feelings, our inner experiences, and not in the realm of nature or of morality. But if that is the case, how do we know that it is *God* that we find, if we find anything to which we feel driven to give that name? Might we not be projecting our hopes and dreams, our fears and our inner drives, on to an imaginary supernatural being? Both philosophical argument and psychological study can produce numerous instances where this in fact seems to be what is happening; can they not be extended further to form an explanation of all forms of religious experience?

And so God retreats. Where to, though, if the general drift of these arguments is accepted? The answer must be: into meaninglessness. For so far we have been talking as if 'God' were a word of accepted meaning which had, together with that which it represents, to be found a place in the world and in the account we give of it. But the problem is rather more difficult. How can this word 'God' be given any meaning if any grounds we give for associating God with areas which

68

are accepted as realities, the natural world, morality, experience, are to be cut away from under our feet by hostile argument? If 'God' seems to break all the rules that govern the way in which we analyse the world and our experience, how can we talk about God and retain a comprehensible meaning in what we say? 'Today, we cannot even understand the Nietzschian cry that "God is dead!" for if it were so, how could we know? No, the problem now is that the *word* "God" is dead.'[6]

The last pages may have seemed somewhat abstract and over-intellectual, if the briefness with which the argument has had to be put leaves them comprehensible at all. To see their relevance, however, we have only to think of many of our own inbuilt assumptions and the assumptions of those around us. For whether the arguments against the existence of God or even the meaningfulness of the word are ultimately true or not, they happen to be the ones which have in practice won the day. They have all had their effect on the way in which Western society has developed, and have by various means found their way, perhaps almost in picture form, into our consciousness and below it. And because our freedom is as it is, the scales are weighted against those who believe in God and want somehow to express their belief.

Belief in God

That sentence was a biased one. It has to be. For at this stage I have to say quite plainly that I myself am quite unable not to believe in God, however meaningless that phrase may be to others. I can see the reasons for not believing in God, I can see difficulties in giving meaning to the word God. There are times when I can be almost completely convinced by them, when my mind just goes round and round in circles at the incomprehensibility of it all. But it is impossible for me to take the final step. Perhaps that is because of my particular conditioning and make-up more than anything else. I do not have any security. I cannot explain my being unable not to believe in any coherent terms that satisfy me, nor, in the end, does my more academic theological training help. I am, in fact, in the position of the listener in the illustration towards the end of Chapter 4, quoted from Deryck Cooke: when it comes down to the fundamental experience I am tongue-tied, either way, and to complicate matters is the nagging question whether the experience is real at all. I only know that to deny God would be to deny the truth. But how to explain this?

I have read only one sentence, put in three different ways by three writers (two of them contemporary with us and the other from nineteen hundred years ago), which has really seemed to reach right to the heart of the question of God. The biblical writer is the author of the Epistle to the Hebrews, who included in his account of faith the words 'Anyone who comes to God must believe that he exists and that he rewards those who search for him' (11.6 NEB); the modern versions are: 'At the centre of the Christian faith is belief in God, and the only ultimately satisfactory ground for believing in God is the fact that God really is, and that the belief is true'[7]; 'It is first necessary to be quite clear about one thing: that is, that there is only one decisive reason for believing in God, namely because *God is*.[8]' Their substance has been drawn out in rather greater lengths at the end of a *Guide to the Debate about God:*

> Either God does not exist or else he must establish his own existence. The believer is, in his heart of hearts, aware of this. For he knows that the debate is not about whether God exists but about how he can be shown to others or hung on to when doubt invades oneself. In reality there are no adequate reasons for God's existence. He is. The atheist also understands this. He does not believe.[9]

But who *is* God? may be the impatient question. What is the point in going on like this when you haven't said anything about what 'God' means? And there is a real problem, for if it is almost impossible to write an account of 'Who am I?', how can we be expected to say anything about 'Who is God?'? But obviously something more, however inadequate, is needed in addition to the single word God.

At the beginning of the period when men were particularly occupied with arguments 'proving' the existence of God, between the eleventh and thirteenth centuries, Anselm, Archbishop of Canterbury (c. 1033–1109) developed a famous proof based on the premiss 'God is that than which no greater can be conceived'. His argument may not do all that he intended, but the terms in which it is phrased can still serve as an indication of the sort of reality to which Christian talk about God refers:

> God is the summit of all possible perfections and then a perfection beyond them. He is more than we can utter, more than we can conceive; the fulfilment, infinitely beyond our hopes, of our deepest longings; the reality, infinitely beyond our conceptions, towards which our highest thoughts are striving. He is the only being who alone is worthy of worship.[10]

It is no good taking the pictures and imagery which the Christian tradition has used of God and pulling them to pieces from the outside. In fact, there is no point in even beginning to look for God if we cannot feel something of the vision to which those sentences point. We have to try to stand in the same position and look in the same direction in which the Christian tradition points, and see whether we are met by the One towards whom we look. For as we have seen, personal terms are unavoidable in talking about God and what we believe to be our experience of him – they arise inevitably when we come to terms with the practice of prayer.

If 'God' has this kind of significance, then it is hard to see how the word can adequately be translated into other terms. In an address which he gave at a memorial meeting for the great Jewish thinker and mystic Martin Buber, the American theologian Paul Tillich remarked that when he was a member of the Religious Socialist Movement in Germany after the First World War, trying to heal the split between the churches and labour, one of his tasks was to replace traditional religious terms, including the word 'God', with others acceptable to the religious humanists who were also members of the moment: 'After I had finished, Martin Buber arose and attacked what he called the "abstract façade" I had built. With great passion, he said that there are some aboriginal words like "God" which cannot be replaced at all. He was right, and I learned the lesson.'[11] Or, in a brilliant illustration from the literature of the tube train: 'There is no substitute for God.'[12]

God, then, is – and we know him to the degree that he makes himself known. But there are two courses that might be taken here. Confronted with the 'Retreat of God' outlined earlier, the dominant trend in much professional theological thinking has been to retreat, too, reducing the area of faith and of the action of God. Theologians have felt it advisable to abandon ground altogether, rather than to risk damage from the many pitfalls that lie in wait, and have made a virtue out of necessity. Their conclusion seems to have been: 'Certainty somewhere – or nothing.' Nature, morality, experience can bring us no certainty – therefore they must be disregarded. We must rest on God alone and what he shows us in a very narrow sphere, beyond all reason. God is God here, no matter what anyone says to the contrary, even if all our other experience points in a very different direction, and we see him nowhere else.

But can we really live in a perpetual divorce of this kind? Is it any wonder that the God who is so constricted, who is not allowed to make an appearance (or, it is said, he would be an idol) in virtually any of our experience, should become undernourished, grow sick and die? We may accept that if God is, we can only know him because he is and shows himself to us. But need this happen so completely counter to our rationality? Might we not expect God, if he is, to leave trace of himself in some areas of our experience? It was the point of Chapters 3 and 4 to show that such an expectation was not as unreasonable as all that. They were an attempt to show, in advance of the main question, that the areas which theological argument rules out for its purposes, may not be as barren as they are sometimes made to appear, provided that we do not ask for too much. To have some knowledge of God through our experience of people, through certain facets of the world, is not, as we have seen, a claim that can be defended with complete success. To attempt to go too far in this direction has its dangers. But the prospect seems much better than the alternative, to give up hope before we even begin.

Belief and Action

This chapter can end with a return to a point made in passing at the beginning. In discussing man's freedom to respond to God, John Hick brought out the element of commitment. Becoming aware of God must make a difference to us, and, conversely, if we are to have a chance of this awareness we may have to embark, in hope, on a new course of action different from anything that we have tried before (this is where the chapter on prayer, which has so many connections with the present chapter, fits in).

But however our awareness of God may grow, the central Christian claim remains that the first step is not, and cannot be, with man. It is crucial to the Christian understanding as it has been expressed in the past that our commitment and our action are a response to what is already there before us. It is because of this particular understanding that Christians have always been so concerned with the past, because it is in past events and particularly in the person of Jesus of Nazareth that they have felt able to see both evidence of this prior action on the part of God, and also something of the kind of commitment which is required of them in return.

NOTES

1. John Hick, *Faith and Knowledge*, Macmillan 1967[2], p. 133.

2. Quoted by Maurice Wiles, 'Looking into the Sun', *Church Quarterly*, January 1969, p. 191.

3. John Hick, *op. cit.*, pp. 133 f.

4. Antony Flew, in Antony Flew and Alasdair MacIntyre (eds.), *New Essays in Philosophical Theology*, SCM Press 1955, p. 96.

5. See, e.g. James Richmond, *Faith and Philosophy*, Hodder and Stoughton 1966; David Jenkins, *Guide to the Debate about God*, Lutterworth 1966.

6. Paul van Buren, *The Secular Meaning of the Gospel*, SCM Press 1963, p. 103.

7. P. R. Baelz, 'Is God Real?', *Faith, Fact and Fantasy*, Fontana Books 1964, p. 47.

8. David Jenkins, *Living with Questions*, SCM Press 1969, p. 38.

9. David Jenkins, *Guide to the Debate about God*, p. 110.

10. David Jenkins, *Living with Questions*, p. 3.

11. Paul Tillich, 'Martin Buber', in John Bowden and James Richmond (eds.), *A Reader in Contemporary Theology*, SCM Press 1967, p. 54.

12. Again David Jenkins, *Living with Questions*, p. 181.

7 Jesus

It may seem odd to have come so far in a book about Christianity with virtually no mention of Jesus. Doesn't an approach like this make things more difficult for itself by starting in the wrong place? Wouldn't a number of the problems we have been considering so far have resolved themselves much more easily if all the elements of Christian belief had been laid out at an earlier stage?

There was more than a tactical reason for leaving out thinking about Jesus until this point. Considering the meaning and significance of his person and work earlier would have involved us in two difficulties which, though still considerable, may not prove so serious now that some background has been laid out.

Jesus and God

First, the Christian claim has, almost from the beginning, been that Jesus is God. Now what Christians have understood by 'God' has been coloured in many ways by what they believe they have seen in Jesus. But it has never been the case, until very recently indeed, that Jesus has had to supply virtually the whole content of the meaning of 'God'. In a recent and influential re-interpretation of the gospel, one American theologian has written, 'Whatever can be known concerning "God" has been answered by the knowledge of Jesus made available in the event of Easter. Whatever "God" means – as the goal of human existence, as the truth about man and the world, or as the key to the meaning of life – "he" is to be found in Jesus, the "way, the truth, and the life".'[1] An approach like this may be attractive and even helpful at a time when, as we have just seen, the word 'God' seems to raise so many problems. But it is so different an approach from the tradition which it claims to be re-interpreting that it amounts to a completely new form of Christianity altogether. 'Jesus is God' is not the same thing as 'God is Jesus'. Those who made the first statement brought with them in their minds some idea what 'God' stood for, and when they applied this word to Jesus, too, it was to put his work in a context where it would be impossible to arrive simply by a process beginning with the human qualities of Jesus and extending a line upwards from there.

So before looking at Jesus, it was necessary to see the sort of content that has been given to the word God, and at the same time to be made aware of just what Christian tradition has been saying in its assessment of this man from the Palestine of two thousand years ago. 'Jesus is God' does not mean that by himself Jesus was the most perfect man who ever lived, that he gave himself more fully than any other man, that his message is, in purely human terms, in a class apart from any other religious teachers. Indeed, if it did mean this, such a claim would be extremely hard to defend. For Jesus without God, Jesus presented in human terms and 'God' in terms of Jesus, is by no means first choice among religious leaders of the past, once comparisons *at this level* are brought into it.

This was made abundantly clear in a broadcast discussion several years ago between two agnostic philosophers and two theologians. If comparisons entered into it, argued the philosophers, some people might indeed be intoxicated by the story of Jesus, but they might well take their pick elsewhere and prefer the Buddha or Socrates as giving them the best approach to live by. Indeed, why restrict oneself to one person? Why not draw on a combination of any or all of the religious teachers who have lived, like Aldous Huxley's *Perennial Philosophy?* Even Jesus' ethical teachings are not, on these terms, either exceptionally original or, by our standards of ethics, exceptionally valuable. They come from the past, they are often very terse and not at all easy to understand and apply, and more often than not they deal with one-to-one relationships without taking into account a man's wider responsibilities.[2]

Jesus is not Jesus without God. Any careful reading of the gospels ought to make that clear. But that need not involve going over to the other extreme, the idea described as: 'Jesus was really God almighty walking about on earth, dressed up as a man. Jesus was not a man born and bred – he was God for a limited period taking part in a charade. He looked like a man, he talked like a man, he felt like a man, but underneath he was God dressed up.'[3] Each of these alternatives is little more than playing about with pictures – without looking more thoroughly to see what underlies them.

But before we go into that, there is the second difficulty to consider. For us, at any rate, Jesus of Nazareth can never be a starting-point. For Jesus of Nazareth is no longer available to us as a point to start from. Jesus was indeed the historical starting-point for Christianity, in Palestine almost two thousand years ago – but to that Jesus we have only indirect access, as to other historical figures of the past. Our first encounter with Christianity may be by being born into a Christian family, by meeting and following Christian friends, by reading about Jesus or even by believing that we are called by him. But any or all of these approaches involve pictures, of one kind or another; whatever our experience of Jesus, it must be different in kind from our experience of other human beings of flesh and blood who are our contemporaries, and the question 'How do I know Jesus?' must to some degree involve the kind of issues which we came up against when we were considering how we know God and the way in which our knowledge of the past is historically conditioned.

Jesus and History

This can be demonstrated easily enough. Suppose that you

gathered together all the available modern attempts to portray Jesus and compared them with each other. The most obvious thing to strike you would be the degree to which they varied among themselves. Jesus would change from book to book, from author to author, varying his colour with his surroundings. For teachers he is the great Teacher, for revolutionaries he is the great Revolutionary, for those who care for young children he is the kind father-figure. For Dietrich Bonhoeffer, he became 'the man of others', for Lord Beaverbrook he was 'the divine propagandist'. And so one could go on. In the best known of all studies of the question 'How can we know Jesus?', *The Quest of the Historical Jesus*, Albert Schweitzer wrote:

> Each successive epoch of theology found its own thoughts in Jesus; that was, indeed, the only way in which it could make him live. But it was not only each epoch that found its reflection in Jesus; each individual created him in accordance with his own character. There is no historical task which so reveals a man's true self as the writing of a Life of Jesus. No vital force comes into the figure unless a man breathes into it all the hate or all the love of which he is capable. The stronger the love, or the stronger the hate, the more life-like is the figure which is produced. For hate as well as love can write a life of Jesus, and the greatest of them are written with hate. . . .[4]

His comments are none the worse for having been made sixty years ago; indeed, what has happened since they were made would seem to bear them out all too well. For with the decline in both the love and hate of Jesus that has characterized the last half-century, so his figure seems to have become more and more colourless, with only the evangelicals and – most recently – the protesters and revolutionaries bringing a new passion.

Writing about Jesus, then, tells us more about the author than the person of Jesus himself. But why is this, and what chance is there of getting to a stage beyond such heightened self-portraiture?

The heart of the problem, as almost any New Testament scholar will agree, is that we simply do not have enough material about Jesus, and that what we do have is already in the form of theological interpretation. Because there are so many unknowns, because there are so many gaps in our information about Jesus, because the exact significance of some of the material that we do possess is unclear, the answers to anything more than a very limited question will be full of guesswork and conjecture. And once that process begins, the temptation to fit the evidence to the conjecture and not vice versa becomes very strong. What line we choose will, in these circumstances, inevitably have a great deal of our own views about it. And this – it is essential to realize – must be from now on a permanent state of affairs, unless (as seems highly unlikely) completely new evidence bearing directly on Jesus turns up.

This position may sound highly sceptical. But it is simply a consequence of looking at the evidence seriously. Something like this would be said by almost any New Testament scholar – and New Testament scholars are, in the end, the only ones with competence to answer the purely historical question. (Though it is amazing how many others are willing to dispute this and claim a direct line to some form of knowledge of this kind not available to the specialists.)

But, it will be argued by those who know something of writings about the New Testament at first hand, isn't it notoriously the case that New Testament scholars differ among themselves? Are not others very considerably more optimistic about the reliability of the gospels? This may be so, but it is – to make the point yet again – not just a matter of optimism or pessimism, but of knowing and not knowing, of having evidence or not having evidence, of being nearer to or further from the truth. And here the best that we can do is to reach some sort of approximation, positive or negative. It may be that a more sceptical view represents a personal tendency towards doubt and distrust and a reluctance to face the full implications of what the gospels say; but it may also be that over-confident reliance on them represents a need for security and reassurance and a reluctance to face the full implications of the fact that the gospels do not say what they were once believed to say. Nothing is gained by bandying epithets here, or by refusing to consider the implications of possible alternative views.

That is not to say that we know virtually nothing about Jesus or that he never existed. Questioning which comes from being soaked in the evidence is very different from the sort of scepticism that is coupled with a refusal to look at any of the facts at all. As we shall see, the more one looks the more there is a real and fascinating mystery about Jesus that confronts us. But it *is* a mystery, and seems very unlikely to surrender all its content. We are unlikely to do more than produce a series of *our* pictures, each in some way conflicting with others, each with its special insights and distortions.[5]

This will happen if we try to make our own historical pictures by means of characteristically modern research. But modern research is little more than two centuries old. If we argue along the lines sketched out above, what are we to make of the experience of the church for the other seventeen hundred years of its existence? What about the other kind of pictures of Jesus which have been held in the past?

Jesus and Doctrine

We must begin by looking at them briefly.

The first thing to notice is that they are not biographical or historical pictures. The reason why we have difficulty in seeing just who Jesus was is because the people of the first century did not ask by any means the same sort of questions as we did. The gospels and the rest of the New Testament do not ask 'Who was Jesus?' in the sense of 'What was he like as a person?' but rather in the sense of 'What is his meaning for us? What has he done?'

Even the gospels are theological portraits in this way rather than anything else, each with its own theological interpretation of Jesus. The direction of interest becomes clear with Paul. Here is a man who lived within twenty years of Jesus, and there is every reason to suppose that he may have known next to nothing of Jesus as a person – at any rate, there are no clear references to Jesus' earthly life in his letters. Instead there is a kaleidoscope of changing pictures and images. Even the name 'Jesus' plays a subsidiary part to the title 'Christ', 'the anointed one', itself a picture with special associations. 'Christ, our paschal lamb, has been sacrificed' (I Cor. 5.7); 'He disarmed the principalities and powers and made a public example of them, triumphing over them in him' (Col. 2.15); 'In him all things were created, in heaven and on earth, visible and invisible, whether thrones or dominions or principalities or authorities – all things were created through him and for him' (Col. 1.16). Paul's 'biography' of Jesus can take barely a verse: 'Descended from David according to the flesh and designated Son of God in power according to the Spirit of holiness by his resurrection from the dead' (Rom. 1.3 f.) – and always in theological terms.

And so it goes on. In the New Testament, the theological terms used are predominantly those of the Old Testament and of Judaism, though there are some Greek ideas too. But as Christianity moved out into the Graeco-Roman world, so the meaning of Jesus was translated into Greek terms and expressed in new pictures – the pictures that are presented in the historic creeds and the classical statements about the person and nature of Christ. But what are these statements in fact saying, and what do their pictures express? They are about the meaning of a person, about the significance of particular events in the past, but they are by now most indirectly related to those events and that historical person. To say that they are about Jesus of Nazareth is not only an over-simplification, it may even be misleading.

Let me try and explain why.

At the beginning of the Second World War, Professor J. M. Creed, a distinguished theologian and New Testament scholar remarked:

To say that Jesus is Lord and Christ is not and never has been simply another way of recording the direct impression of his historic personality. It is a synthetic, not an analytic judgment, an affirmation of faith about God, Man and the World, no less than an affirmation about the historic Jesus of Nazareth.[6]

In other words, talk about Jesus is often not only talk about *Jesus*, but talk about God, man and the world. But it might be possible to go a step further and say that much Christian talk has sometimes, even in the classical period of Christianity, been *not so much* talk about Jesus as talk about God, man and the world in the light of what men have believed Jesus to be. Talk about Jesus has been a way of putting into words thoughts about religious experience and about how things are.

This is the context in which many pictures have been used to illustrate 'Jesus'. But at this point an important question arises. How far does Jesus control the pictures that are used to portray him, and how far do the pictures that we use of Jesus control our idea of him? How much do we read out of Jesus, and how much do we project on to him? How much of theology has been a matter of saying, 'If Jesus was and in actual fact did this and that then the following conclusions are to be drawn . . .' and how much of it has been a matter of saying, 'From our experience and knowledge of the world we recognize that this and that quality are supremely good; Jesus was supremely good, therefore he must have had these qualities'? It is impossible to do much more than raise the question here, but it is a crucial and a disturbing one. For it can be used to harness all the emotional force behind the word Jesus to endorse a particular view of life. This is what can clearly be seen to have happened in some of the more modern lives of Jesus: the writers tried to combine recreating Jesus as he once was with constructing a figure considerable enough to serve as an object of faith. Their failure is obvious from the pages of Schweitzer's book with its series of mirror-reflections of the views of nineteenth-century man. But how far is what the fathers of the church did in their doctrinal constructions of the significance of Jesus completely different in character? How can we be sure that some of their views were not similarly mistaken? In other words, may it not be that some of the classical pictures and images used in the doctrine of the person and work of Christ are, instead of being pictures of Jesus, pictures of a theological or philosophical understanding of Jesus, set rock hard and taken as an absolute? 'Jesus is the eternal, fully divine, second person of the Godhead made flesh, therefore ...' 'Jesus is the final revelation of God therefore ...'.

Creeds and Finality

Christians pride themselves on the Creed of Nicaea, and it is an important and vital document in its context. But it also created serious problems. One patristic scholar has put it like this:

The psychological impact of the historical moment of Nicaea (AD 325) was enormously influential. Even in the days of persecution the Church had regarded the imperial powers that were as ordained of God; and then, almost overnight, God's vicegerent was to be found no longer persecuting but presiding over the largest and most representative gathering of bishops in the Church's history. Surely such a body in such a situation would be guided not merely to see the next step forward but to provide a firm and lasting answer on the fundamental issue of the Church's faith. ... Looking back at it from the vantage point of fifty years later it stood out as a rock, different in kind and in quality from any other statement of Christian doctrine. Here was a God-given fixed point in a world of such doctrinal giddiness that a fixed standing ground was the most obvious thing which one would be likely to ask God to give.

Now this was precisely the moment at which ... the problem of the nature of the incarnate person of Christ was coming up for more detailed discussion and debate. And for this stage of the debate it is no longer true to say that everything was in a state of flux. Now there was a fixed starting-point. The problem of Christ's person could be posed in one way and in one way only. It was the problem of how the second hypostasis of the Father, whose eternal, fully divine, distinct existence was already known and affirmed, had become man. However difficult the problem might prove – and it could hardly have proved more difficult than it did – there could be no going back on the terms in which it was posed.

We are so used to the incarnational problem being posed in this kind of way that we normally fail to see that there is anything particularly odd about it. It seems after all a reasonable enough procedure in a complex piece of business to settle one issue first and in the light of that decision to move on to the next issue. But it perhaps sounds less self-evidently reasonable if we alter the analogy and speak of fixing irrevocably one term in the solution of an equation before the sum has been solved or indeed been shown to be patient of any solution on that assumption.[7]

May not the creeds themselves, once intended as pictures of the nature of Christ, be barriers to a proper understanding because they have been prematurely made absolutes, not themselves been examined?

The same approach can be made to the theme of the 'finality' of Christ, the idea that he is the once-for-all, unique revelation of God, which had led to so much over-confidence on the part of Christian believers and so much arrogance, misunderstanding and hostility to the non-Christian religion. Is this idea, which is still used so vigorously as a standard for measuring attempts at picturing the person of Jesus, like the creeds, also a hindrance to understanding? These questions are put as questions, to prompt further reflection, but it should be pointed out that there are indications that the argument should be put in an even stronger form.[8]

Who is Jesus?

To return, however, to the pictures that we have of Jesus. One further point still has to be made. Suppose, for example, we had a full and historically accurate picture of Jesus? What would we see, and how would we be helped?

The more we learn from historians about the way all human existence and activity are relative to some particular cultural environment, the less can we expect that any human figure will be equally acceptable to different cultures. Jesus must have exercised attraction over many in his day, or there would have been no Church. It is hardly to be expected that if we, with our very different cultural background, could see him exactly as he was we should find him speaking to our condition in the same immediate way.... I am not suggesting that

84

any picture of Jesus is likely to emerge in which he is revealed as essentially wrongheaded or in any way morally repugnant. What I am prophesying – very tentatively – is (that if we had this fuller picture we should see) a figure who because he belonged fully to the first century cannot belong in the same way to ours.[9]

This brings us back to the quotation from the historian Carl Becker which appeared in Chapter 2. We may be able to understand something of Jesus, but our connection with him, as with any figure of the past, must be an indirect one. Because we are so historically minded, we have to look at him in historical terms. And in doing so, we cannot exclude the possibility that we may, the more we come to see of what he was, have increasing difficulty in relating Jesus to our own day.

There is a pernicious short cut which assumes that once we have a picture of what the historical Jesus did and said, all we have to do is apply the lesson straight to our day. This is too facile. For what Jesus did and said was – to risk tedium by repeating yet again – said in terms of his own situation and time and not ours. We no longer think in the framework within which his message was expressed, nor can we – even if we make the effort. Just as the New Testament translates the meaning of Jesus into other terms, so must we, with the difficulty that there is no accepted language that we can use today. That, more than anything else, is our problem – and it will take some time to solve.

The way to it will have to be a complex process involving a number of things. It will include looking at what can reasonably be said to be our historical knowledge of Jesus; it will include looking at the first pictures of him as presented in the New Testament, which stand nearest to him in time of all the evidence we possess. It will include looking further at the pictures developed from these first pictures, seeing the kind of arguments used in their construction and the evidence on which they are based. And all this will have to be done taking into account what we know of reality from other areas with which we are familiar.

The heart of the Christian claim is that Jesus is God. As we look at the gospels, at what we can see of Jesus and the way in which he is presented, at the character of his life and death and, above all, at the event we call the resurrection, lying between the death of Jesus and the belief of the early church that he was alive and in their midst, we may see the meaning of this claim more deeply. But, as was said at the beginning of this chapter, we will not understand it properly without more profound thinking, not only about what we mean by Jesus, but about what we mean by God. Without some coherent thought about the nature of God, it seems highly unlikely that the pieces which form the elements of the Christian tradition will add up to a convincing unity. Once again, Jesus is not Jesus without God.

This discussion may seem highly sophisticated, sceptical and even abstruse. And of course all the issues brought out in it cannot be pursued by every Christian. But because they seem to be involved in the question of the truth about Jesus, someone must tackle them at some point and draw the conclusions. Too much talk about Jesus these days is far too vague and emotive to mean anything to more than a very narrow group of people. Even to ask 'What am I talking about?' every time the words 'Jesus' or 'Christ' were mentioned would be a useful and not too arduous self-discipline. Surely we owe it to the truth to put what Jesus means in clearer terms than many of the all too familiar clichés – and once we begin to do that there is no avoiding the problems.

Of course, many people *are* directly attracted by the picture of Jesus in the gospels and feel drawn to live their life in the light of that. Many are converted, sometimes quite suddenly, by pledging themselves to a 'Jesus' of this kind. But if what has been said here is at all true, this Jesus is only a provisional picture, and unless there is constant reflection on the nature of this picture, a development forward from and beyond the first conversion, taking in an understanding of 'God, man and the world', the same damage may be done as by any of the other unexamined pictures that we may have, and in a more subtle way.

At this point we are on the edge of a great mystery. Like the question of God, the question of Jesus has a strange power to grasp and to hold us, a power which never ceases to surprise. But this power lasts in its authenticity only so long as it is allowed to retain its mystery, and is not misused by those who seek to extend their personal 'certainties' into areas where it is no longer legitimate to press them.

A recent, longer study of *Who is Jesus Christ?* has ended with some wise words, and one of the most moving quotations about Jesus from our own time. Both will bear repeating again here.

> ... Our handling of the question about Jesus Christ cannot be separated from the continually changing understanding which we have of ourselves and of the world – an understanding which derives not so much from passive inspection as from the experience of, and reflection upon, these deeds. There is therefore an ineradicable element of mysticism, though a mysticism of action, about our search for the identity of Jesus Christ. The often quoted conclusion of Albert Schweitzer's *The Quest of the Historical Jesus* indicates vividly the place where, above all, the question about Jesus Christ is to be asked:
>
> 'He comes to us as One unknown, without a name, as of old, by the lake-side. He came to those man who knew Him not. He speaks to us the same word: "Follow thou me!" and sets us to the tasks which He has to fulfil for our time. He commands. And to those who obey Him, whether they be wise or simple, He will reveal Himself in the toils, the conflicts, the sufferings which they shall pass through in his fellowship, and, as an ineffable mystery, they shall learn in their own experience Who He is.'[10]

NOTES

1. Paul van Buren, *The Secular Meaning of the Gospel*, SCM Press 1963, p. 147.

2. James Richmond, *Faith and Philosophy*, pp. 190 f., gives an outline of the broadcast.

3. J. A. T. Robinson, *Honest to God*, p. 66.

4. Albert Schweitzer, *The Quest of the Historical Jesus*, A. and C. Black 1954[3], p. 4.

5. Anyone with strong views on this subject ought to read F. Gerald Downing, *The Church and Jesus*, SCM Press 1968, very carefully.

6. J. M. Creed, *The Divinity of Jesus Christ*, Fontana Books 1964, pp. 10 f.

7. M. F. Wiles, 'The Doctrine of Christ in the Patristic Age', in Norman Pittenger (ed.), *Christ for Us Today*, SCM Press 1968, pp. 85 f.

8. See A. O. Dyson, *Who is Jesus Christ?*, SCM Press 1969; M. F. Wiles, *The Making of Christian Doctrine*, Cambridge University Press 1967, 'Looking into the Sun' (see Ch. 6, n. 2).

9. Dennis Nineham, 'Jesus in the Gospels', *Christ for Us Today*, pp. 61 f.

10. A. O. Dyson, *Who is Jesus Christ?* pp. 123 f.

8 The Bible

'Have you read your Bible today?' asked the Wayside Pulpit outside my Underground station on the day this chapter was begun. And it added, 'The Word of God endures for ever'. Both the question and the text, however, are based on rather too simple assumptions: that the Bible ought to be read every day, and that it is essentially unchanging. Rather more might be said than that.

To begin with the question; for most people the answer will have been a definite 'no'. To look at a familiar subject in a new perspective, at the beginning of October 1969, the French magazine *Elle* published an interview with a M. André Froissard, who was making a new translation of the Bible into French to be sold by instalments, fully illustrated, on the news-stands. He was asked whether he thought people still read the Bible in 1969, and replied: 'No, hardly anyone reads it. According to our enquiries, half the people have never opened the Bible, forty-five per cent hardly know it; they have read Genesis, or Psalm 103 (used at funerals) or the Song of Songs, because they think it's sexy .... Only five per cent have really read the Bible.' And there follows the picture of the unapproachable book, now made far more accessible in its modern translation and format.

M. Froissard is optimistic about his new translation, but he might be less sure of its long-term prospects were he familiar with the scene in this country, where there has been a flood of new versions over the past ten years or so. For despite this continuing activity, there is little evidence that new translations have brought about much of an increase in Bible reading. Indeed, figures from some of the Bible-reading societies indicate that here, as in so much else, Christianity is on the decline.

Knowledge of the Bible is more often than not knowledge at second hand, superficial knowledge, and whether the old picture of the differently bound book with all the little numbers down the page and the double columns remains, or whether the paperback *Good News for Modern Man* and the like have displaced it, the Bible remains to all intents and purposes a book apart. It is dismissed or revered, argued over, held at the taking of an oath, but hardly read.

Nevertheless, it is still widely thought of as 'the Word of God'. Most Christians want to assert this in some sense or other, and non-Christians feel cheated unless they, too, can assume that this is what Christians believe. But despite this belief in the permanence of the Bible, the fact is that the Bible has not always been in existence, nor has quite the same degree of importance been attached to it at all times. There was a long period when the Jewish people lived and worshipped without a holy book; that only came into being at quite a late stage in their history. There was a period when the Christian church existed without the New Testament, and debated whether it really needed the Old. There was prolonged argument over which books belonged in the Bible. Even when the Bible as we know it was accepted by the church, the understanding of it varied. The idea that 'the book of mysteries was also an encyclopedia which contained all knowledge useful to man, both sacred and profane',[1] an idea which lasted in many circles right up to the beginning of the nineteenth century, was slow to develop. The idea of the infallibility and inerrancy of the Bible, paradoxically enough, seems to have reached its height at a time when it was most difficult to defend; earlier biblical scholars were quite happy to acknowledge errors of one kind or another.

Nobody really believed in the verbal inspiration of the Holy Scriptures until the geologists began to question it. Hitherto, broadly speaking, people believed everything they read in the Bible, in the

90

same way that some people believe everything they read in the newspapers.[2]

Methods of interpreting the Bible have varied quite extraordinarily in twenty centuries or so. The Bible has presented a changing face to changing circumstances. It is not as permanent as might appear at first sight. Nor, when it is read closely, is it entirely reconcilable with some of the views that have been held about it.

The Problem

The Bible is usually regarded as the book with a difference, the holy book. Precisely what the difference is between the Bible and other books has been explained in several ways. Sometimes a traditional view of the authority of the Bible is still kept; it is the divinely inspired, authoritative guide to Christian conduct and belief, containing a timeless oracle from God, giving advice and information and inspiration to readers of any generation. Sometimes the uniqueness of the Bible is described in more sophisticated terms. Although it is a product of the past, it contains the record of certain events and ideas which, when understood properly, are a basic guide to the present. Sometimes the stress will be on the clarity and simplicity of the Bible, sometimes the problems it raises will to some extent be acknowledged. But the fundamental presupposition seems to remain the same. The Bible *is* different, it *is* set apart, it contains answers for us, and it is worth studying – because it is the Bible.

Many familiar activities are based on this assumption. The Bible is regularly read aloud in churches and daily in morning prayer and evening prayer by many clergy; sermons are preached on the basis of biblical texts; doctrinal statements are grounded on what the Bible is believed to say. There are countless schemes of Bible reading sponsored by one organization or another. And all this is possible without raising in any fundamental way what the Bible is. It can be carried on simply on the old assumptions and pictures of the nature of the Bible.

91

But are they true? Are we justified in taking them for granted? Can we be content simply with the question 'What can the Bible say to me?' Suppose for a moment that we forget these assumptions of the Bible as a different, holy book, a book set apart, with special authority, then what do we see?

Those who have investigated the Bible with this aim in mind have found a whole host of problems, which have, if anything, been made more acute rather than less with each new translation (excluding paraphrases, which beg the question) that has appeared. When we really come to grips with what the Bible is saying, sentence by sentence, it is neither at all obviously an authoritative holy book for us, nor a book which has a clear message which speaks to us today. On the contrary, the more accurately it is translated, the more thoroughly it is read with an effort to understand it in its own terms, the more it can be seen to be what it essentially is: a collection of books from a different, past world. There are some passages that can make the same impact on us as any great poetry or literature from the past, but there are far more passages which are incomprehensible, irrelevant, and for all practical purposes quite unusable.

To see the real difficulties that the Bible presents, the person to talk with is a teacher. It is one thing to pick and choose from the Bible to preach sermons, to use it as a vehicle for some sort of devotional meditation, to read passages from it, again selected, to a congregation which can be counted on to display no obvious reaction. It is quite another matter to have to teach the Bible regularly to a class of schoolchildren who are all too ready to question what they hear and to explain the meaning that actually arises from the Bible in a way which satisfies them and the teacher's own integrity.

The Bible belongs first and foremost to its world, and we belong to our world, and the gap between the two amounts to a great chasm. Between the Bible and us lie two thousand years of history and a whole revolution in thinking. The assumptions with which we approach the Bible are not the assumptions that the Bible itself has, and at times it seems that the only way in which the two can be reconciled is by leaving one set aside altogether.

It seems more and more difficult to fulfil the principles which have governed the teaching of 'Scripture' almost continually in England since they were first put forward by the London School Board under the terms of the 1870 Education Act:

> The Bible shall be read and there shall be given such explanations and such instructions therefrom in the principles of morality and religion as are suited to the capacity of children.[3]

A College of Education lecturer in Religious Studies has commented:

> Most of the School Boards followed the London example and this, in effect, was the beginning of 'Scripture' in maintained schools. There were some at the time, and there were many in the succeeding generations, who were aware that there was more to religious education than familiarity with the words of the Bible. In the classroom, however, the tyranny of 'Scripture' has too long held sway. Now, it seems, thanks to the findings of the developmental psychologists, 'Scripture' is finally out – at least from the primary school – and thematic teaching ('the slow building of experience as the basis of religious experience') is in.[4]

The teacher's frustration may be put like this: It is possible to begin with the Bible and its world and to try to understand that. Strides may be made in picturing the Near East of the tenth century BC or the Palestine of the seventh century BC or the Mediterranean world of the first century AD. With luck, pupils may be brought to see something of how the men and women pictured in the Bible lived and what their environment was. But how is this world of so long ago to be connected with our own? Is there any direct link between the concerns of the Bible and the way in which they are expressed and our own concerns and the way in which they are expressed, short of tacking on some relevant 'moral' where it seems appropriate? Furthermore, concentration on the passages that do seem to have some 'message' quickly brings boredom through over-repetition.

Thematic teaching is an attempt to solve the problem by turning it upside down. Instead of beginning with the Bible and working forward from that, some of the newer syllabuses for religious education begin with the world of present human experience and try to work back from there to the world of the Bible. They take 'themes': 'fire', 'water', 'bread', 'health', 'families', 'money', 'books', 'roads', which relate to the experience of children (and adults) and approach the Bible through them. But in practice this can prove to be exchanging the frying pan for the fire. Efforts of this kind run up against the difficulty that more often than not the Bible has little direct and distinctive to offer that could not be brought in more naturally from elsewhere. Where points of contact can be made, they tend to be superficial:

> Why use the Bible to illustrate the fact that 'Foxes have holes and the birds of the air have nests' – particularly as the rest of the sentence ('but the Son of man has nowhere to lay his head', Luke 9.58) is, presumably, not to be used at this stage? Why refer the infant teacher to the cursing of the barren fig-tree in order to establish that fig trees grew in Palestine? Are a string of Bible references needed to show that there was reading and writing in Bible times, that certain trees grew in the Middle East or that various animals were common in Bible lands?[5]

At worst, the Bible is distorted because the emphases are placed quite differently in this new approach from those in the Bible itself; the Bible is bent to modern experience rather than being allowed to speak in its own right.

It might fairly be retorted that teaching the Bible to children raises special problems. That is quite true. But they only differ in degree, not in kind, from those which face adults. And as adults have commended this new approach, it must be assumed that they do not believe it to be too out of tune with their own understanding of the place of the Bible.

Interpreting the Bible?

Whatever the case, however, does it not seem that even this

94

newest of approaches is only the latest in a long line of attempts to do *something* with an often rather problematical book which for Christians just happens to be there? In the past the Bible may have played a more dominant role, but a variety of attempts at interpreting it may be seen to be as much rooted in the present experience of the interpreter as in the Bible itself (if not more so).

Most sermons are still good illustrations of this. The preacher does not usually develop his text by doing more accurate historical research into its background. He brings to the Bible his own concerns and questions and those of his congregation and tends to read them into what he is preaching. He may do his best to let the Bible speak for itself, but this is hardly practicable. For the meaning that is extracted from a text depends on the questions that are asked of it, and in a sermon it is hardly possible to put the sensitive questions that are really demanded. The sermon is filled out with the preacher's own experience, and the richer that is, the more the sermon speaks to us. (For an illustration of this, it is worth reflecting on one of the best collections of sermons I know, Harry Williams' *The True Wilderness*.)

Very much the same thing happens with the larger works of theology which turn to the Bible for material for their arguments. More often than not the author has his own approach, his own questions which shape the particular enquiry which he is making, and he applies them to the Bible and reads out the result. Of course, when this is done the answers that emerge are not totally unrelated to the Bible; they are different from what they would be if the Bible had been ignored altogether. Moreover, the Bible played some indirect part in shaping the thought of those setting out to interpret it in this specific way. But can their conclusions really be claimed as what 'the Bible says'? (It would be an interesting exercise to take some modern books of systematic theology, particularly some of the more 'popular' ones—e.g. Harvey Cox, *The Secular City;* Paul van Buren, *The Secular Meaning of the Gospel;* Jürgen Moltmann,

Theology of Hope—and treat them in the same way as Schweitzer treated the 'Lives of Jesus'. How much is read out, and how much is read in?)

Again, many people read the Bible regularly by means of devotional commentaries or notes, in which a passage is chosen for each day of the year and a message attached to it. The passage selected for reading in one well-known series, the day I write this, is the scene in St Luke's gospel where Jesus is rejected (Luke 4.16–22, abbreviated!), and the thought suggested for it is: 'How often selfish emotions and shallow thinking cause men to spurn the message, and turn on the messenger sent by God.' But how far does this really look into the meaning of what Luke was trying to portray? The danger is that this kind of approach trivializes the meaning either by over-simplifying it or by applying it in a direction for which it was not originally intended.

The examples given above are from modern uses of the Bible, but the same methods of interpretation can be traced back right through Christianity and even to Judaism. Given a 'holy book' belonging to a different age, the problem of how it is to be understood by later generations who think in different ways will always arise, simply because of the ongoing course of history and the constantly changing perspectives it brings with it. Statements made in a way which is bound up with the world view of one age cannot be directly taken over, any more than they can be directly argued with, without being altered from their original meaning. And this makes the question of the 'truth' of the Bible just as difficult as the question of the 'truth' about Jesus which we considered in the previous chapter.

The Contribution of Criticism

In view of this, it seems clear that, whatever the difficulties, the *primary* way in which we should expect the Bible to speak to us today is in an indirect way. It cannot be looked on primarily as a book with an immediate message for the individual person, for the present, but must be seen as part of a continuing tradition reaching down to the present. Our question must be, here as elsewhere, 'What must the truth be, and have been, if it appeared like that to men who thought and wrote as they did?'[6]

This involves us in a critical view of the Bible and therefore in the work of historical-critical scholarship, a generally unpopular subject. The biblical critics have acquired a bad name for themselves (and, generally speaking, the more probing the questions they ask, the worse the name) as those who have undermined faith and introduced the serpent doubt and generally brought about confusion into the uncomplicated person's mind. Even the word 'honest' cannot be used these days without other connotations, but this is in fact what they have been, and their enquiries have been much more positive than is generally accepted.

The results of criticism are certainly negative if the main concern is to see how much of the old pictures and assumptions about the Bible they have left standing. What critics have discovered will, if taken seriously, demand a very great deal of rethinking of these familiar ideas. But their positive achievement can be put like this.

We can now see, with a reasonable degree of certainty, the way in which the Bible, Old and New Testaments, came to take the form it now has. We can see something of the way of life and historical fortunes of the people who appear in and who wrote the Bible, from the second millennium BC to about the beginning of the second century AD, and we can see the way in which this life and history was interpreted. We can begin to see, in the approximate way which is the best result that can be achieved by a historical investigation, how the minds of the writers of the various books of the Bible worked and the significance of the imagery and pictures that they used. We can see, for example, how Matthew's theological portrait of Jesus differed from that of Mark or Luke or John; how Paul's view of Christ and the Christian life differed from that expressed in letters wrongly attributed to him (I and II Timothy and Titus) and 'letters' written by other early Christians. Instead of a holy book all on one level, we have a variety of people in a historically changing world, and at their centre the mysterious historical person of Jesus himself, and all that happened to him.

Furthermore, as we look more deeply at this world, we see that it is not ruled off by a neat boundary and confined within the pages of the Bible. There are books in the Bible which might well have failed to find a place in it; and there are books outside the Bible which, but for certain historical circumstances, might have found their way in. The Bible is surrounded by blurred edges; it has no obvious shape.

But if this is the case, are we justified in laying so much stress, explicitly or implicitly, as we do on the Bible as the holy book? Does this not land us in precisely the same difficulty over the actual content of the Bible as we saw in the previous chapter occurs if too much stress is laid on the creeds? The mere idea of the 'holy book' can close our eyes and our minds to what the Bible actually says. Too much Bible reading of the wrong kind can even be misleading. The desire to make the Bible speak straight to us can prevent us from ever seeing how carefully and how profoundly thinkers and writers of the past reflected on the events that they were writing about.

Revaluing the Bible

What has been said in the previous paragraphs must inevitably sound derogatory to the Bible. It is not meant to be, but when so much superficial praise is lavished on it, anything less must seem very negative. Perhaps the main theme of the chapter might be translated into terms familiar from the financial world like this. For too long the Bible has been so over-valued that its position cannot be credibly maintained at the current rate. If no attempt is made in future to maintain this official rate, but the Bible is allowed to 'float' and find its own level, it may prove to have considerably more value than is supposed by those who speculate against it. [7]

The same thing has been put in a much more scholarly way in a paragraph which is worth most careful thought:

> Would it not have been better, and would it now be better, for the church to be content with saying, 'Here are these books; we believe them to be profitable books from experience; they have come out of the lives of some of us and they express something of our faith; they are all we have, let us get on with it'? Is it, after all, so obvious that the Christian faith was meant to have a holy Scripture in the sense of the Old Testament, which it succeeded in demoting but fatally took as its model? Granted that the written text is strong precisely where tradition is weak, that as a fixed text it is less prone to corruption and more capable of acting as a purge, are these more than debating points, as good in their way as the debating points from the other side that it is the church which decides the canon and that Scripture does not interpret itself? Do they have to be blown up into a doctrine of holy authoritative Scripture? Granted also that such a Scripture has affected reform in the church, notably at the Reformation, did it do so without grave distortion, and except as achieving its immediate and necessary aim was not the Reformation something of a disaster, and nowhere more so than in its belief that it had achieved a fixed doctrine of the position of Scripture in the church? And is it to be assumed automatically that what Scripture did before it will necessarily do again, and that in its make-up it is fitted for this? Has not reform in our own time come from other sources, and included not only reform by the word of God but reform of the word of God?[8]

We need the Bible, for what it tells us about the events which gave rise to Christian belief, for what it tells us about Jesus, for what it tells us about the formative part of the tradition in which Christians stand. And if we look at it in the new ways which critical study has made possible for us, we shall find that it once again takes on new life.[9] Critical study makes clear how much the Bible is also tradition, chapters from a story which goes on beyond its last pages down to our own time, and with less emphasis on the Bible itself – and consequently not so much time continually spent covering the same ground – there will be more opportunity for looking more closely at the chapters of the tradition which lie between the time of the Bible and ourselves. The present-day wholesale ignorance of the many different ways in which Christians have lived and interpreted the world between the time of the Bible and the present, brought about very largely by an over-long retention of the view that the Bible and the Bible alone is all that the Christian needs, does us no good. And with more knowledge of the Christian tradition over the centuries, we might be helped to a better understanding, not only of ourselves, but also of the whole Christian community, the church.

NOTES

1. Beryl Smalley, *The Bible in the Middle Ages*, Basil Blackwell 1952, p. 26.

2. Charles Smyth, *Church and Parish*, quoted in D. E. Nineham, 'Wherein Lies the Authority of the Bible?', *On the Authority of the Bible*, SPCK 1960, p. 88.

3. Quoted by Donald Horder, 'Symposium: The New Agreed Syllabuses', *Learning for Living*, May 1969, p. 17.

4. *Op. cit.*, p. 17.

5. *Op. cit.*, pp. 18 f.

6. Leonard Hodgson, *For Faith and Freedom*, SCM Press 1968[2], pp. 87 f.

7. I owe this illustration to a meeting of lecturers in Religious Education from colleges in the Bristol area to which I was invited in October 1969.

8. C. F. Evans, 'Tradition and Scripture', *Religious Studies* 3 (1967), p. 336.

9. For a fuller version of the position suggested in this chapter see John Bowden, *What about the Old Testament?*; T. G. A. Baker, *What is the New Testament?* (both SCM Press 1969).

9 The Church

One of the oddest, most unattractive aspects of organized Christianity is its arrogance, its blind certainty that what it says and does is right and brooks no alternative point of view. When I became a Christian it happened because to begin with I had been moved by the charity and confidence of one priest. I had never before come upon anyone so relaxed, so unworried about religion, and I could see that out of the supreme certainty it gave him he could be more generous than most people to those who disagreed with him. There was no need to harangue people, to judge them, to needle them; God to him was a fact about life and he proceeded to live in acknowledgment of it; a phenomenon which moved me as few things in my life have moved me.

It was a long while, however, before I could bear to consider that this individual priest was part of the Church, and the reasons for this are not far to seek. My impression of the Church ever since I could remember anything was a very different one. I remembered all those snippets in the newspapers where they quoted a sermon or article written by a reactionary vicar, all those reported statements of archbishops and bishops; in most of them one thing shone clear – a thinly-veiled distaste for people and society and underlying the distaste a cold fear.[1]

Monica Furlong's feelings will be those of many people who either discovered or rediscovered Christianity in the way she describes. And her remarks already give some idea of how difficult it is to write about the church. For on the one hand there is something so wrong with the church that it makes one want to attack it with an almost overpowering bitterness (I wrote several pages in this vein to get it out of my system and then tore them all up), while on the other there are so many good, sane, astonishingly kind, believing people in it that none of the harsh generalizations can really be made to stick completely.

101

No one who has ever worked in a parish can ever sneer at the church and what its members do, however great the faults may seem. For in any parish, even the most unprepossessing of them, there will always be numerous unpublicized, almost unnoticeable ways in which members of the church are living up to their title 'the body of Christ', believing and acting on their belief, often in the most difficult of all conditions. And yet – no one who has ever worked in a parish can ever forget the pettiness and the triviality and the frustration which seem constantly to be there.

Facts and Fears

Part of the trouble is, of course, that the churches are hopelessly hindered by the mould into which history has cast them. If earlier we have been considering how history is constantly on the move, changing ideas and attitudes, now we have to take into account the other side of the picture, that once those ideas and attitudes take concrete form in bricks and mortar and stone, whether attractive or unattractive, they set hard and cramp and distort the change that is necessary for life. The Christian churches have inherited a ridiculously large number of buildings belonging to different groups. all being propped up by a rapidly diminishing number of people, and prevented from being combined and made more usable by differences, coming from well back in the past, for which there are now more often than not few rational grounds. Anyone who wants to bring about a change has his hands tied by the past almost before he begins.

It would be more excusable that so little progress is being made if there were more signs of some realization of how much the duplication of church and chapel, the interdenominational tensions and squabbles, were damaging the work of Christians. But even when that is talked about, so relatively little is done. Again, within the local congregation it is so often possible to feel that there is a solidity about the very structure of the community which reaches into the past and cannot, will not, change whatever may happen in the world. Even sparsely attended churches manage to generate an atmosphere of security, that there is all the time in the world, and that it is only necessary to hold fast.

And yet, on the other hand, where attempts are being made to reshape the church or bring the churches together, the picture is often even worse. Whatever the merits of the rewriting of canon law, the reports on the redeployment of the clergy or changes in their training, the most obvious thing about them that emerges at a glance is that they have no soul; that they are just like the reports of any other institution – but with one difference. In the reports of other institutions the relationship of the organization to the purpose it serves is usually quite plain; when it comes to the church, it seems possible to move in some circles of administration for years without the slightest explicit recognition of what the church exists for or how it began.

Time and again, reading what tends to be printed in the church newspapers and said in church assemblies and conferences of one sort or another one is given the impression, like Monica Furlong, that the church is simply concerned with remaining what it has become. It has resigned itself to being an organization, and its interests and its business both are, at this level, those of an organization: financial, administrative, social. It is bad form to snipe at the organization by criticizing it from within, by being a 'dismal jimmy'; that is disloyalty to the company. Commercial language has even been taken over to the extent of talking about a new 'image' for the church. It is not very long since *The Times* carried a series of articles on new trends in marketing groceries, one of which dealt with the problems of a dated institution with a number of rebellious, stubbornly independent and unco-ordinated sub-branches, and attempts made to give the concern a face-lift. Only with difficulty could one realize that this was not one more article about the church; it was, in fact, about the Co-op.

103

Whatever other factors may be involved, one cannot but feel behind all this the chill of the fear mentioned at the end of the quotation that opened this chapter, a fear to look more deeply because of what might be there. And it is a fear that can be sympathized with. For all the changes of attitude that have been touched on in this book, the advance of science and what that it has led to, the social changes which have altered so many of our patterns of living, the increasing difficulties for religious belief, taken together represent a challenge greater than that faced by any other body. And those who have, on a traditional understanding of the church, been the ones responsible for facing it, the clergy, have had in addition to cope with a threat to their own status. Many of them are no longer at all clear about what their role in society is.

As a result of these problems, the all too familiar picture has emerged. There are increasing signs of refusals of people to identify themselves with the organized life of the church, which have accelerated rapidly in the last few years. The number of baptisms and confirmations has dropped almost like a stone, church attendances have fallen, and above all, fewer candidates are offering themselves for ordination and an increasing number is leaving the parish ministry for other employment, either through frustration or a feeling that under present conditions their work is irrelevant. Of those who remain, many are worn out and disheartened, doing little more than serving out time.

These are the facts and the fears. And the only way of dealing with them is by facing them. But what could be expected? How might the church fit into the wider picture that we are attempting to see?

The Church and its Members

There can be no question of drawing up a blueprint for the ideal church, without taking into account what already exists. That would only add one more form of the church to the many that we already have, and introduce one more division. The problem is much more straightforward. Can anything be done to build up within the present church and the structure it now provides a new, more flexible form which will have a better chance of survival when the old one is past repair – as seems most likely to happen if the present trend continues? Is it possible to get to the heart of the question of what the church is and to find an answer that reduces the depression, tension and frustration that are all so obvious in it at present? Here, at any rate, are some brief reflections, even if they don't get very far.

First, the church is people, responding to God as the Christian tradition has come to see him, in the way that the rest of this book has outlined. Because the Christian tradition is people, because (as we saw) we come to know and be ourselves in community, because, too, community is essential if putting belief into practice is to be more than a series of isolated personal efforts, the church is an indispensable element of Christianity. At the same time, the church is all its members, not just part of them (this has been said for ages, but to all intents and purposes 'the church', at least the one to which I belong, seems still too dominated by clergy and a pseudo-laity). What the church is doing is not just what committees or commissions or ecclesiastical spokesmen or church organizations are doing, but includes the work of Christians wherever they are. Similarly, what the church thinks and believes and teaches is not just what its clergy say in an official capacity; it includes the work of teachers in schools and lecturers and professors in universities and colleges whether they are teaching pupils, doing research or talking together in conferences.

The time is past when the 'teaching of the church' could be summed up in short statements with authoritative force. A case might just be made out for certain statements on matters of discipline (though there are obvious dangers and difficulties here), but if our approach to and knowledge of God has anything like the character suggested by this book, the best that the church can offer is help in showing what the problems are and how they might be overcome. The picture of the church as a shelter from disturbing thinking and a haven of reassurance may be an attractive one, but in an open society like our own, deluged by all the apparatus of mass communication, it is irrevocably out-dated and doomed to failure.

This need not be a bad thing. For if the insights of Christian belief are essentially true insights into how things are, then Christians have nothing to fear from questioning. And there are encouraging signs that despite all the questioning which is still going on, through the work of the wider church a new, if less spectacular, confidence is emerging.

The Role of the Clergy

But if more stress is to be laid on the fact that the church is all its members, there must be some corresponding change in the understanding of the clergy. For while there may be a widespread feeling that 'clergy are less than men', as can be judged from the way in which they are so often caricatured, within the church they are still the people who have the power, without whom even some of the simplest actions (like distributing the bread and wine at the communion) cannot be done.

Already in the third century Christians began to complain that bishops were becoming unmindful of Jesus' words that those who would be first must be servants of all; and later bishops and presbyters came to regard their authority in terms of personal power, received from Christ and the apostles by delegation when they were consecrated and ordained. This notion of power dominated the mediaeval theology of the ministry, and it is far from dead. It is held, for example, that at the Last Supper Jesus delegated to his apostles his priestly powers of offering the sacrifice of the mass, a power that has come down by unbroken succession to validly ordained priests today. At another time, it is said, Jesus gave them the power of granting or withholding absolution; at another time the authority to teach, the powers of *magisterium*; at another time he gave specific power to Peter only. As far as delegation in succession to the apostles is concerned, the disputes between Roman Catholics and Anglicans have in the past centred, not on whether there has been ... 'a lineal descent of power from the Apostles by continued succession of bishops', but on the exact nature of this power, on whether Anglicans have this succession, and on the question whether or not the papal power is to be included in the same category. [But] this whole way of understanding the ministry is vitiated by the fact that the New Testament writers are not concerned with institutions in the later sense at all, and that Jesus himself eludes any pretentions on our part to grasp him in our religious categories. Yet it still underlies much contemporary theology of the church, and in particular any view which, recognizing the centrality of the sacraments to the church's life, makes these sacraments and thus the church itself depend wholly on the ministry.[2]

The change in attitude that is needed is in the direction of a view that recognizes much more clearly that nothing shapes a man more than what he does, his training and his work. Instead of seeing 'priesthood', 'ministry' as something conferred on a man, giving him special powers, ministry needs to be seen in the light of what a man actually does. And what he does will be determined, in the case of the church, by his own gifts and the needs of the time. Where it is still possible to run parishes usefully along traditional lines, there will still be a need for people trained for the work that they must expect to find waiting for them there. But it is being realized more and more that parish life is not the only form of church life, and that other, more varied means of expressing the presence of the church are also needed, the leadership of which may need different characteristics and different training.

The Local Church

This brings us on to a second important question. What form should the church take in today's world? Community life is much more flexible than it used to be. People divide their life between home and work, often a considerable distance apart, and may live in many different places during their lives. In some areas, the traditional parish may still take in a distinguishable social community; in others, particularly in the cities, it may be a quite artificial unit and have no relevance to community life.

107

In his book *The Secular City*, the American theologian Harvey Cox sums up the problem:

> The difficulty is that we are not moving from one stage of society in which a particular form of church life, the residential parish, was the characteristic form, into a stage in which some other form of church life will replace it. The situation is far more complex. The key word to describe what is happening in our society is *differentiation*. We are moving into a stage in which we will need a widely differentiated range of different types of church organization to engage a society which is becoming differentiated at an accelerated rate.[3]

What this may mean is difficult to sum up briefly, but some of the problems that will need to be dealt with may be mentioned.

The chief needs of the church in meeting together are to worship, for people to meet each other, to grow in understanding what being a Christian means and to be instruments for doing whatever work in a particular community can best be done by church members. At present, in many places the framework within which this happens is all too formal. Even with revised orders of service, the usual pattern of regular worship with hymns and Bible readings and sermons and set prayers is insufficient by itself to fulfil all the functions it is supposed to perform. It cannot serve as a focal point of man's response to God which stirs his imagination and insight, a meeting place, a period of instruction and a base for the work of various organizations, and do all these things properly. Yet that is what happens in so many places, with the one weekly meeting perhaps supplemented by extra activities of semi-official organizations.

On the whole, it would seem that too much stress is laid still on regular 'going to church' and too little is made of other possibilities, not least that of meeting and talking in each other's homes. A more simple form of Sunday services (and in many cases fewer of them), coupled with a far more flexible complex of worship, discussion, friendship and activity might make all the difference. The occasional more elaborate service or the performance of something new and quite different, whether it is Britten's *Noye's Fludde* or *A Man Dies*, which needs a good deal of preparation and rehearsal can have (as has been shown) a whole variety of by-products. The only thing that needs to be avoided is the trap of combining worship and other activities at too superficial a level, so that the result is a mockery to the best both in modern culture and the Christian tradition (some of the activities of 'pop' hymn-writers seem to fail very badly here). People are much more sensitive to what is authentic and what is not than many churchmen seem to realize.

There are limits to what can be done if the clergy are regarded as those who are responsible for all the arrangements, but if there is much less of a distinction between clergy and congregation and between regular congregation and those who are not members of it, again experience shows that surprising results can be achieved. Loneliness, a desire to talk at more than a superficial level without being thought odd, are far more prevalent than we imagine, and what begins as no more than doing something together or even simple hospitality can develop into deep and lasting ties and friendships. But considerable openness is needed at the beginning.

What will happen to the churches over the next ten years or so is anyone's guess. It may well be that in some places the churches will lose most of the characteristics by which we know them today, that the crisis of their institutional collapse and the fear in which they are gripped may cause them to smother still further the possibilities of new life that they contain. But what happens in this respect is in the end of secondary importance. All that matters is that there should be people somewhere, somehow, who even in the most modest, temporary and continually changing groups go on attempting to be the church. And here Monica Furlong's vision is as moving as the thoughts with which the chapter began:

Within the strange, sprawling, quarrelling mass of the churches, within their stifling narrowness, their ignorance, their insensitivity, their stupidity, their fear of the senses and of truth, I perceive another Church, one which is really Christ at work in the world. To this Church men seem to be admitted as much by a baptism of the heart as of the body, and they know more of intellectual charity, of vulnerability, of love, of joy, of peace, than most of the rest of us. They have learned to live with few defences and so conquered the isolation which torments us. They do not judge, especially morally; their own relationships make it possible for others to grow. It does not matter what their circumstances are, what their physical and mental limitations are. They really are free men, the prisoners who have been released and who in turn can release others.

There are more people like this in the churches than outsiders ever imagine, and meeting them is never a surprising or unnatural experience, like catching a glimpse of Stylites on his pillar. This, one knows, as soon as one has seen it, has a naturalness about it, a rightness, a sweetness that one would give anything to share. To see it is to know that this is how one ought to be, only somehow it went wrong, and one got lost instead in the muddle of worry and work and people and money.

If the Church could offer this kind of fulfilment to more people, it would be doing the work of healing and preaching the gospel which is what it exists to do.[4]

NOTES

1. Monica Furlong, *With Love to the Church*, Hodder and Stoughton 1965, p. 23.

2. Victor de Waal, *What is the Church?*, SCM Press 1969, pp. 105 f.

3. Harvey Cox, *The Secular City*, SCM Press 1965, p. 157.

4. Monica Furlong, *op. cit.*, p. 22.

10 Who is a Christian?

And so we come to the question that started it all. Who is a Christian? It should be clear by now that there is not going to be a straight answer. It is difficult to see how there can be. But various threads can be drawn together.

If we look back over the way we have come, two things emerge. First, many of the things about which Christians have been so confident and dogmatic in past times are by no means as straightforward as they have believed them to be. Many of the familiar pictures, ideas, assumptions, statements are no longer enough in the form in which they have been retained. What we can see of the realities towards which they point needs new expression more appropriate to the way in which we talk and write and think in our particular period of history. I hope it has been clear that this is not to say that the substance of traditional Christianity is, or has been, just plain wrong – a conclusion which is regularly drawn whenever there is any move towards a restatement of Christian beliefs. Any understanding of the sense of history which is the new dimension that has been added to our thinking over the past century will show that that, too, is a gross oversimplification. The point is more subtle. It is a matter of saying: 'People have made these kinds of affirmation in the past within the context of a world-view which it is no longer possible for me to share. Their affirmations were intimately bound up with that world-view of a bygone age. They are therefore for me no longer live options; I am not in a position either to affirm them or to deny them; I cannot give any satisfactory sense to them *in that form*.'[1]

There are signs that a view of this kind is at present a minority opinion in the church. Others would be more confident. Were the fortunes of the church better at the present time one would be rather more impressed by this confidence. As it is, one can only suggest that the kind of difficulties expressed by both teachers and pupils in schools, colleges and universities, where the bulk of serious theological thinking and discussion seems to be being done at present, indicate a need for the minority opinion to be stated much more widely and taken into account.

Church, Bible, God, Jesus, all have to be given less positive descriptions; but they are still there, as realities that do not give way completely even under the most stringent questioning. Perhaps the question of each needs to be approached rather differently now; perhaps the certainty and assurance of the past is no longer possible in anything like its old form. But there is enough in the exploration of the consequences of what has been said here to provide a faith to live by.

Is there not more? Of course there is. In a subject so large and so demanding it is impossible to put into words all that one knows, and that on certain occasions one realizes one knows; and it has been a central theme of this book that any single view will only show up part of the reality. But what we do not yet know we do not yet know, and there is no point in someone else brandishing it at us in the form of doctrinal statements from the past and saying, 'But that's part of Christianity, and you've left it out'. Surely it is more important to build up, and make one's own, certain insights into Christianity which make sense in the realization that there must be more to come, than to have an obsession about past standards of belief simply because they have been valued in the past? Certain actions, certain statements may have been necessary for the preservation of the truth of Christianity at particular times in the past – it does not automatically follow that we need carry them around with us for ever.

112

In his book of sermons *The True Wilderness*, Harry Williams describes how he decided, alongside teaching academic theology, to ask to what degree a doctrine of the creed or a saying of Christ had become part of what he was:

I resolved that I would not preach about any aspect of Christian belief unless it had become part of my own life-blood. For I realized that the Christian truth I tried to proclaim would speak to those who listened only to the degree in which it was an expression of my own identity. Previously, it seemed to me, I had often been like a man who, while perhaps he enjoyed a good tune, was essentially unmusical and who attempted from the books he had read to describe the quality of Beethoven's quartets. And I wondered how much I had thereby contributed to the emptying of the churches by making the Christian gospel appear unreal and irrelevant to people's lives.

This, he in fact found, was not so much resolved by him as decided in some area beyond his control. And he goes on to describe the result:

The result is not so much intellectually unsatisfactory as intellectually unsatisfying. The intellect craves for complete systems of explanation set out with logical coherence. . . . But there are areas of human life where explanatory systems can falsify as well as illuminate. Personal relations are an obvious example. . . . What is true of personal relations is *a fortiori* true of man's relationship with God. Systems of explanation illuminate up to a point and then falsify. And when the attempt is made to gather up the totality of man's experience of God within the confines of some systematic orthodoxy, then the falsification can be considerable. What is being described here is not intellectual error. It is that the wine of life cannot be contained within the bottles of intellectual definition and if we stick to the bottles, failing to perceive that they have been burst by the wine, then we find ourselves with no wine.[2]

Not only the trouble facing the churches, but the positive and appreciative way in which *The True Wilderness* was received suggests that this is an authentic way forward for Christianity. We begin from where we are.

The second thing to emerge from the way we have come is the confirmation of the fact that the wine has indeed gone and is being found elsewhere. Whatever conclusions we may draw about the ultimate significance of the various areas of experience we considered in the early chapters and the reality behind them, it is more than obvious that these are in fact the areas which claim people's interest and attention when they are interested in anything. To go on to take the view of them that has been outlined here is again very much a minority opinion. Others would be far less confident, indeed would rule out such a view altogether. Again, however, were the fortunes of society and the general quality of personal experience and understanding richer, one would be rather more impressed. There is enough evidence to suggest that part of the problem is that ultimate questions are being avoided, that here too dogmatic opinions set up almost in opposition to religious belief are perpetuating half-truths at the expense of the real truth.

While the second half of this book has been apparently negative (more negative than might be expected), then, the first half has been more positive – more positive than I expected before the pieces were put together. The consequences of this emphasis, in retrospect, might be put like this. Half the trouble with Christian belief is that by insisting on the pattern of proclamation and assertion, of speaking before listening, it finds itself put in the dock and questioned about its statements by others. But the dock is not a very good place from which to ask questions in return, which is what most needs to be done. It would be far more satisfactory for all concerned if there were more possibility of genuine conversation.

Conversation, however, is hindered by many of the kind of unexamined assumptions, pictures and labels that we looked at in the first chapter. And the one that is particularly our concern is the label 'Christian'. If it is brought too much into the foreground it can get in the way of proper contact and understanding and action. 'Is this Christian?', 'Is he a Christian?', 'Am I letting Christianity down?' And of course to the non-Christian, the very word (rather like the clerical collar in some contacts) can immediately give the wrong impression.

Thus there are times and places where the question 'Who is a Christian?' is quite irrelevant; where simply by being persons, ourselves, we will learn far more about people, our world – and about God – than we would otherwise. In the situation which has been described in this book it becomes more and more difficult to draw any kind of dividing line between those who are Christian (in the wider sense that their view of the world has much of the quality of the best of Christianity) and those who are not. This is not an attempt at a conversion by definition; it is simply an indication of how pointless certain concerns to identify Christians can be.

Dietrich Bonhoeffer wrote in his *Letters and Papers from Prison*, with all the excitement of someone who has made a new discovery: 'To be a Christian does not mean to be religious in a particular way, to make something of oneself (a sinner, a penitent, or a saint) on the basis of some method or other, but to be a man.'[3]

What is the Difference?

But does that mean that being a Christian is reduced to conforming to one of the meanings that the word has had, according to the dictionary, since 1577: 'Human; decent, civilized, respectable; a presentable person.' Are Christians no more than men of good will?

The question has been raised acutely by the new emphasis on social, international and racial concern within Christianity coupled with the public uncertainty about God and the possibility of religious belief. The title of this book was in fact prompted by the questions of a churchwarden after he had read Bonhoeffer and when he was being confronted with some of the recent slogans from the British Council of Churches such as 'Let the world write the agenda'. 'It's all very well,' he said, 'this talk about Christians being men, and I understand just what it's getting at. But what I want to know is, what is the difference between Christians and others?'

If what I have been saying is true, then being a Christian

will not necessarily show obviously on the outside. The cliché 'You can be a good Christian without going to church' is probably true of more people now than it has ever been. The kind of life to which Christianity points is not always easily identifiable; the label does not always guarantee the product, nor does the product always bear the label. The point is far too familiar to need dwelling on.

Where the difference surely comes, however, is in what might best be called the realm of 'self-understanding'. It comes in what Christians understand themselves to be, the interpretation they put on the world, the perspective they bring to it. This perspective will be determined by many things and it will be determined slowly and indirectly. In the chapter on prayer, we saw the importance of making decisions, 'responding out of imaginative, sensitive, integrated, many-sided awareness of the time, event and question', built up out of a 'coherent, generously conceived structure for living'. What is true in the case of prayer is also true of Christianity as a whole. What we make of prayer, of God, of the Bible, of Jesus Christ in developing our understanding will shape us (if we let them) over the years into ourselves in a way which would not happen without them. We can see this in other people; we may hope that it will happen in ourselves. Such a process will not necessarily mean that the outward appearance of our lives appears very different from those around us – the decisions we come to, the sacrifices we make or do not make, our personal efforts may be (and these days so often are) put to shame by those with no religious or Christian beliefs at all. But that does not mean that the difference in understanding is negligible. For it is, in the end, the intangibles that make all the difference to life. After the more theoretical questions we have looked at, it is time to come to a more practical level. So I end with pointing to two things that can be found in Christianity as – in my experience – nowhere else.

The first of them is joy. In our preoccupations with the problems facing Christianity, the problems facing the world, the problems of our own lives, it is easy to be too preoccupied with tragedy, to miss a joy that is more than cheap enjoyment, a conviction that despite everything else, *nevertheless* it is possible, through God, to rejoice without superficiality, without mockery, without avoiding the real issues. When we stand in the Christian tradition, we are led back, through all the uncertainties, to God and Jesus, to the cross and resurrection, to that which when taken with all the other realities impresses itself as being as real as any of them. For all its modern neurosis about the reality of the *fact* of the resurrection of Jesus, the church has not been very good at showing the quality of the resurrection life – it is far better at Lent – perhaps with some justifiable fear of lapsing into sentimentality or cheapness. But this new quality of life is to be had, at a price, and on the rare occasions when it comes on us we can recognize it for what it is.

The second thing is hope.

Hope beyond Evil

The most nagging question of all has been left to the end, the question of evil. A presentation of Christianity in terms of our becoming fully what we are is all very well, but what about the rest of the world? What about the countless millions who are born and live and die without the chance of even beginning to explore the riches and depths of being a human being? If we can only express Christianity in such narrow terms, does it leave anything for those outside? Is not the point of the great vision of traditional Christianity that it embraces the whole world and the whole of history, and all that is to come, and not just a particular group of people? Has this universal hope vanished for good?

There is, of course, no positive answer that we can give. And perhaps it would be better if we did not even try. Everyone talks far too much these days, and the comforting, optimistic clichés come pouring out at the slightest provocation. In such circumstances, it may well be best for us, first of all, to say nothing: simply to be there. Talking platitudes about suffering can be a very good way of avoiding being involved in it; looking firmly at reality and seeing afresh the inexplicable dimensions of evil will at least prevent our sensibilities from being blunted.

That does not mean that we cease to believe in the ultimate triumph of God, of good over evil; but we may begin to see just how amazing is the faith we dare to have – and how much it must be a matter of *faith*. Because it is faith, and is *our* faith, it will inevitably be fragile and fluctuating. There will often be times when it is difficult to see far into the future. Faith and hope come – and they go.

The way in which faith and our ability to express it vary so much depending on ourselves, the situation in which we find ourselves, and those to whom we may have to speak, is disconcerting and yet strangely reassuring. Ian Mackenzie has described this variation in connection with the question of the resurrection:

After a theological programme on TV, an old lady wrote in to say how disappointed she was that the (eminent) theologian had dodged the question of the Resurrection. I wrote back at length defending him, and laying the usual pseudo-theological smokescreen about this not being perhaps the right way to look at the question, etc., etc. She wrote back saying, 'Do you believe in the Resurrection?' I wrote back saying, briefly, 'Yes'. She wrote back an impassioned letter making two points: first that she was grateful for a direct reply, which clergy all her life had avoided giving, secondly now she felt free to go on *searching*. In other words, a positive answer, *at that moment*, liberated her.

As a result of this experience, ABC TV began our long-running series 'Looking for an Answer', in which viewers sent in thousands of questions.

One of the clergy who dealt with them was a bishop who took the area of life after death. One of the questions was from the woman whose correspondence I quoted, asking 'Will I see my husband again?' I held my breath. To my profound relief, the bishop said 'Yes'. Never was there a less evasive reply.

Imagine my chagrin when a letter arrived from the lady. She was furious. She had been watching the programme in a roomful of friends.

They all felt her question had not been taken seriously, and she was bitterly disappointed. I must say I felt ingratitude could hardly go further. The resources of a major TV company had been mobilized to put out a whole series on the national network so that she would at last have an unevasive answer, and the Bishop had given a convinced and totally affirmative reply. But, *at this different moment*, that was not what she wanted. The simple answer did not liberate.

There are times when, for me also, the Resurrection is an answer; and there are other times when it is a question, which needs a great deal of exploring.[4]

Now there are those of us who are required, by the liturgy of the church and by the duties of a minister, to make promises like that of the resurrection. Sometimes these promises may be made in formal public worship; sometimes they may seem called for in private, for those who are dying and those who mourn. Sometimes they come easily to us – but do they mean anything to those to whom we are speaking? Sometimes they are almost impossible to pronounce without sounding superficial in the face of human tragedy (and therefore, as I have suggested, are better not said). But there are those times when these promises become so true that they can be spoken in the conviction that things could not be otherwise, and this certainly takes in the whole of the situation in which we find ourselves. In moments like this we can see again that there is God, that he is for us. And that is why the very fluctuation in our faith is reassuring as well as disconcerting. For what we have in this way shows itself to be given, given from outside and beyond us. Here is a slender enough basis, but in the strength of it we can hope and expect that what we see of the working and purpose of God cannot stop with us, but has to go on to take in the whole world, and life beyond.

There are some remarks of an English mystic which have stuck in my mind ever since I first read them. Her name was Julian, and she lived the life of an anchoress, a hermit, outside a church in Norwich almost six hundred years ago. In a state of ecstasy she had a series of visions, on which she meditated for twenty years before she set them down in writing. This is at the heart of what she saw:

> Also in this He shewed me a little thing, the quantity of an hazel-nut, in the palm of my hand; and it was as round as a ball. I looked thereupon with eye of my understanding, and thought, 'What may this be?'. And it was answered generally thus: 'It is all that is made.' I marvelled how it might last, for methought it might have fallen to naught for littleness. I was answered in my understanding: It lasteth, and ever shall last, for that God loveth it. And so All-thing hath the Being by the love of God.
>
> In this Little Thing I saw three properties. The first is that God made it, the second is that God loveth it, the third that God keepeth it. But what is to me verily the Maker, Keeper, and the Lover, – I cannot tell; for till I am substantially oned to Him I may never have full rest nor very bliss; that is to say, till I be so fastened to Him that there is right nought that is betwixt my God and me. . . .
>
> It behoved that there should be sin; but all shall be well, and all shall be well, and all manner of thing shall be well.[5]

NOTES

1. Maurice Wiles, 'Looking into the Sun', p. 199.

2. H. A. Williams, *The True Wilderness*, Constable 1965, pp. 8 f.

3. Dietrich Bonhoeffer, *Letters and Papers from Prison*, SCM Press 1967, p. 198.

4. Ian Mackenzie, *New Christian*, 8 August 1968, pp. 14 f.; I am also indebted to his article 'Plea for Necessary Silence', *The Times*, 16 June 1968.

5. Julian of Norwich, *Revelations of Divine Love*, ed. Grace Warrack, Methuen n.d., chs. v, xxvii.

For Further Reading

The variety of books mentioned in the footnotes provide a more than adequate programme for further reading if anyone wishes to follow up at greater length some of the questions that have been raised. So I am mentioning only one book here.

If I were settling on the traditional desert island and could take only one work of modern theology with me, the book I should choose would be Leonard Hodgson's *For Faith and Freedom*, which was republished by the SCM Press in a one-volume edition in 1968. It is now almost fifteen years old, but on each re-reading it comes out as freshly as ever. And little of it needs to be changed, despite the so-called 'theological revolutions' that we have been through in the last ten years. Of course there is much in it to be argued with and disagreed with, but it still seems to me to be a model of how a large-scale piece of theology should be written – some of the profoundest thoughts alternating with as splendid a collection of anecdotes and illustrations as one could hope to find.

Index